J 973.7
B

SIEGES
THAT CHANGED THE WORLD

ALAMO

CONSTANTINOPLE

DIEN BIEN PHU

MASADA

PETERSBURG

STALINGRAD

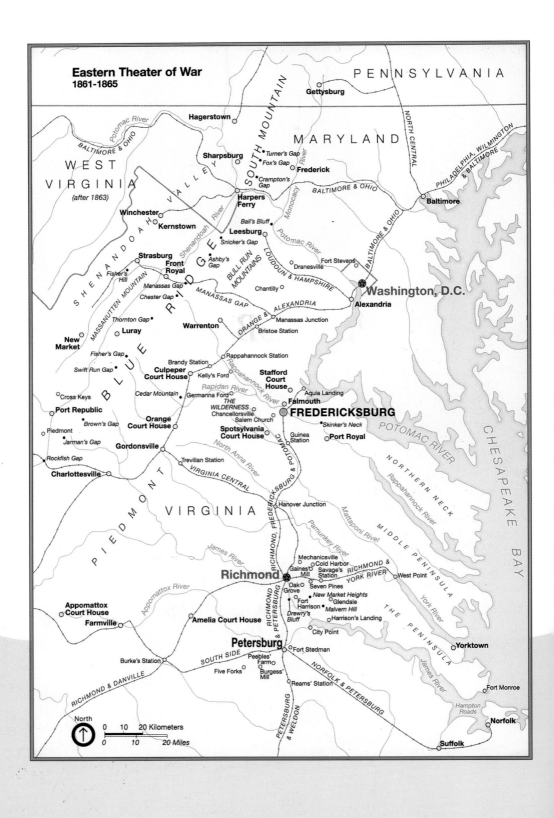

Eastern Theater of War
1861-1865

PENNSYLVANIA

Gettysburg

Hagerstown

MARYLAND

WEST VIRGINIA
(after 1863)

SOUTH MOUNTAIN

Sharpsburg
Turner's Gap
Fox's Gap
Crampton's Gap
Frederick

Potomac River
BALTIMORE & OHIO

Monocacy River

BALTIMORE & OHIO

PHILADELPHIA, WILMINGTON & BALTIMORE

NORTH CENTRAL

Baltimore

Harpers Ferry

Winchester
Kernstown

Ball's Bluff
Leesburg
Snicker's Gap

Shenandoah River

Strasburg
Front Royal
Fisher's Hill
Manassas Gap
Chester Gap

Ashby's Gap

BULL RUN MOUNTAINS

LOUDOUN & HAMPSHIRE

Dranesville
Fort Stevens

Potomac River

BALTIMORE & OHIO

Washington, D.C.

Chantilly

Alexandria

SHENANDOAH VALLEY

MASSANUTTEN MOUNTAIN

BLUE RIDGE

Thornton Gap
Luray

New Market
Fisher's Gap

Swift Run Gap

Cross Keys
Port Republic

Brown's Gap
Piedmont
Jarman's Gap

Rockfish Gap

Charlottesville

MANASSAS GAP

Warrenton

ORANGE & ALEXANDRIA

Manassas Junction
Bristoe Station

Rappahannock Station

Brandy Station
Culpeper Court House
Kelly's Ford

Cedar Mountain
Germanna Ford

Rapidan River

Rappahannock River

Stafford Court House

Aquia Landing
Falmouth

THE WILDERNESS
Chancellorsville
Salem Church

Orange Court House

Spotsylvania Court House

Guinea Station

Gordonsville

Trevilian Station

VIRGINIA CENTRAL

North Anna River

PIEDMONT

VIRGINIA

James River

Richmond

Hanover Junction

Pamunkey River

Mattaponi River

MIDDLE PENINSULA

Mechanicsville
Cold Harbor
Gaines' Mill
Savage's Station
Oak Grove
Seven Pines
New Market Heights
Glendale
Malvern Hill
Harrison's Landing

RICHMOND & YORK RIVER

West Point

York River

THE PENINSULA

Appomattox Court House
Farmville

Appomattox River

Amelia Court House

Fort Harrison
Drewry's Bluff

City Point

RICHMOND & PETERSBURG

Petersburg

Burke's Station

SOUTH SIDE

Five Forks

Peebles' Farm
Burgess' Mill

Reams' Station

Fort Stedman

NORFOLK & PETERSBURG

James River

Yorktown

Fort Monroe

Hampton Roads

Norfolk

Suffolk

POTOMAC RIVER

CHESAPEAKE BAY

NORTHERN NECK

Rappahannock River

Skinker's Neck
Port Royal

FREDERICKSBURG

RICHMOND, FREDERICKSBURG & POTOMAC

PETERSBURG & WELDON

RICHMOND & DANVILLE

North

0 10 20 Kilometers
0 10 20 Miles

PETERSBURG

*Active and continuous operations of all
the troops that could be brought into the field,
regardless of season and weather,
were necessary to a speedy termination of the war.*

—General Ulysses S. Grant, July 1865

BRUCE L. BRAGER
Series Consulting Editor
Tim McNeese

CHELSEA HOUSE
PUBLISHERS
A Haights Cross Communications Company

Philadelphia

FRONTIS The Eastern Theater of the American Civil War—1861–1865

CHELSEA HOUSE PUBLISHERS

VP, NEW PRODUCT DEVELOPMENT Sally Cheney
DIRECTOR OF PRODUCTION Kim Shinners
CREATIVE MANAGER Takeshi Takahashi
MANUFACTURING MANAGER Diann Grasse

STAFF FOR PETERSBURG

EXECUTIVE EDITOR Lee Marcott
PRODUCTION EDITOR Jaimie Winkler
PICTURE RESEARCHER Noelle Nardone
SERIES & COVER DESIGNER Keith Trego
LAYOUT 21st Century Publishing and Communications, Inc.

A Haights Cross Communications Company

http://www.chelseahouse.com

First Printing

1 3 5 7 9 8 6 4 2

Library of Congress Cataloging-in-Publication Data

Brager, Bruce L., 1949–
    Petersburg / Bruce L. Brager.
        p. cm.—(Sieges that changed the world)
Summary: Describes the details and significance of the Virginia Civil War
battle called the Siege of Petersburg.
Includes bibliographical references and index.
    ISBN 0-7910-7100-6 HC   0-7910-7530-3 PB
    1. Petersburg (Va.)—History—Siege, 1864–1865—Juvenile literature.
2. Virginia—History—Civil War, 1861–1865—Juvenile literature.
[1. Petersburg (Va.)—History—Siege, 1864–1865. 2. Virginia—History Civil
War, 1861-1865.] I. Title. II. Series.
E476.93 .B73 2002
973.7'37—dc21

                                                            2002012915

TABLE OF CONTENTS

The Siege Opens

Never had the army been in a better strategic position than it was getting into this fifteenth of June.

—Historian Bruce Catton

On June 12, 1864, three years after the start of the American Civil War, Union forces quietly began to withdraw from Cold Harbor, Virginia, and head south toward Petersburg, Virginia. The men took a route that curved east, away from the Confederates, before turning and heading south. Confederate Commander Robert E. Lee anticipated a Union move, probably one that would continue the Union pattern of the last five weeks, trying to swing around the Confederate right flank.

This time, however, Lee planned to do more than just ensure the temporary survival of his army by keeping in front of his enemy. Lee was going to try to catch Union General-in-Chief Ulysses S. Grant and his Army of the Potomac in motion. Lee hoped he would catch the Union troops when they were most vulnerable, as they actually crossed the Chickahominy River, north of Richmond, Virginia. A Northern victory in the Civil War was not yet inevitable. Lee still had the potential to score a major victory, and perhaps change the course of the war.

Grant was taking a risk to move in front of Lee, get to the supply center of Petersburg first, and cut Lee off from his supplies. According to historian Noah Andre Trudeau:

> The course Grant had determined to follow was a daunting one, requiring disengagement along an almost ten-mile front, a march of nearly fifty miles across swampy, ravine-rippled ground, and the bridging of a tidal river where it was a half-mile wide. To further complicate matters, the crossing place could be reached by Confederate gunboats from Richmond.

Grant's move surprised Lee so much that Lee went ahead with a planned diversion. On June 13, 1864, Lee sent Major General Jubal Early and his 2nd Corps northwest into the Shenandoah Valley to clear out Union troops under Major General David Hunter. When Hunter retreated into West Virginia, Early took his corps all the way to Washington, D.C. In early July, U.S. President Abraham Lincoln watched some of the fighting at Fort Stevens, then on the outskirts of 1864 Washington, but well within the limits of the city today.

On June 14, 1864, Grant notified his chief of staff (best described as the chief administrator of the army), Major General Henry W. Halleck, that the move was going well. In a brief but complete telegram to Halleck, which he assumed would be given to President Lincoln, Grant told Halleck: "Our forces will commence crossing the James to-day. The enemy shows no signs yet of having brought troops to the south side of Richmond. I will have Petersburg secured, if possible, before they get there in much force. Our movement from Cold Harbor to the James River has been made with great celerity and so far without loss or accident."

The next day, Lee had still not detected the Union move. Union troops from the XVIII Corps, cavalry, and so-called "colored" units (African-American soldiers led by white officers) from an X Corps division were approaching Petersburg. The African-American division had never seen combat. Its troops had been stationed at City Point, the main Union supply base on the James River. The XVIII Corps, under General William F. "Baldy" Smith, had been borrowed from the Army of the James, a second Union army that was moving toward Richmond and Petersburg from the east. Smith was in command of the entire force, at least until the expected arrival later that day of the II Corps, under Major General Winfield Scott Hancock.

At 6:00 A.M., Smith's force met Confederate resistance at a place called Baylor's Farm, several miles northeast of Petersburg. The Southerners there held up the Union advance for two hours.

Smith's men finally arrived at Petersburg by about 2:00 P.M. Rather than attack the Confederate positions immediately, Smith decided to take a careful look first. Smith decided that the positions were strong but under-manned. Still, Smith was determined not to attack until he was fully ready. Two weeks earlier, Smith's men had been rushed to attack at Cold Harbor and had been slaughtered. Smith did not wish to repeat this mistake.

Smith may have been a bit overcautious, but when his attack began at 7:00 P.M., it was quite successful. His troops

Major General Winfield Scott Hancock, seated, with his three division commanders, in this photograph taken May or June 1864. From left to right, standing, they are Brigadier General Francis Barlow, Major General David Burney, and Brigadier General John.

took nearly a mile (1.6 kilometers) of trenches, including nine fortified positions known as redoubts. By 9:00 P.M., Smith's first attack ended. The general thought his troops were becoming disorganized, and he did not want to press his luck. He chose not to attack further.

After a slow, day-long march on June 15, Hancock was informed that he needed to hurry to get to Petersburg. He arrived about 9:00 P.M., just as Smith's first attack was ending. Even though the Confederates had received reinforcements, the Union forces still had more than twice as many men in the area. Rather than order an attack with his superior and still fresh forces, Smith did not act. He simply asked

Hancock to have the II Corps take over the positions held by the XVIII Corps and the African-American troops.

If he had been in his prime, Hancock, one of the more aggressive Union generals, and senior to Smith, would most likely have overruled Smith and attacked. Hancock was not in his prime, though. He had not yet recovered fully from a serious wound he received a year earlier at the Battle of Gettysburg. The wound caused Hancock a lot of pain and sapped his initiative. He deferred to Smith's wishes.

That night, Hancock's men had an unusual reaction to their orders. Exhausted from six weeks of almost constant fighting and heavy casualties, the soldiers might have been relieved when they were told to rest. Instead, they sensed that a chance was at hand to end the entire war with just one more attack. They may have been right. Many of the men remarked that night, "Put us into it, Hancock, my boy, and we'll end this damned rebellion tonight."

The soldiers were outraged when they learned that no attack was to be made that night, despite the fact that the odds were much more to their advantage than would be the case if they attacked a few days later, after Lee's army arrived. One Union veteran later wrote, "The rage of the enlisted men was devilish. The most bloodcurdling blasphemy I ever listened to I heard that night, uttered by men who knew they were to be sacrificed on the morrow. The whole corps was furiously excited."

Confederate General Pierre G. T. Beauregard, in command of the defenses of Petersburg, recognized the opportunity the Union troops had that evening. After the war, he wrote, "Petersburg at that hour was clearly at the mercy of the Federal [Union] commander, who had all but captured it, and only failed of final success because he could not realize the fact of the unparalleled disparity between the two contending forces." Smith and Hancock seemed to be the only ones on the scene who did not recognize the opportunity before them.

Beauregard asked Lee for reinforcements. Lee refused. He did not believe the attacks on Petersburg were Grant's main effort. Later that evening, Beauregard pulled one of his divisions from the lines blocking the Army of the James. Beauregard now had about 14,000 men with whom to try to hold the extensive Petersburg lines. He was still out-numbered, and the Bermuda Hundred defenses were far weaker, but time was running out for the Union forces to achieve a quick victory.

June 15 was not the first time Petersburg had been involved in the American Civil War. Petersburg played a role in the war long before the city became a battlefield. Young men from Petersburg went to fight in the war, as did men from most Southern communities. Petersburg was more important because of its location. The five rail lines that served Richmond, the capital of the Confederacy, from outside Virginia met in Petersburg. A sixth line ran from Richmond northwest to the Shenandoah Valley. (Only one rail line went directly from Petersburg to Richmond.) Its position as a railroad hub made Petersburg the supply center for the Confederate Army of Northern Virginia. Capturing this town would deal a major, and probably fatal, blow to Lee's army and to the entire Confederate government.

There had already been one Union effort to take Petersburg. On May 5, 1864, a 15,000-man Union force, under the command of General Benjamin Butler, landed on a peninsula called Bermuda Hundred. Formed by the intersection of the James and Appomattox rivers, Bermuda Hundred was just five miles (eight kilometers) north of Petersburg. Butler was supposed to support Grant by striking at—and taking—either Richmond or Petersburg. With most Confederate soldiers in Virginia with Lee, 65 miles or so away, Butler should have been able to seize either city.

An influential Northern Democrat before the war

started, Butler was one of the first "political generals" appointed by Lincoln to gain the support in the North that he needed to have any chance of winning the war. Butler had some successful moments. It was Butler who came up with the idea of referring to escaped black slaves as "contraband of war." This clever move used the Southerners' own claim that slaves were property to make it legal for the Union to effectively free slaves by confiscating the property of those Southerners who were making war on the government.

Butler had far more political than military skill, however. By June 1864, Butler had managed to get his army bottled up at Bermuda Hundred, held in place by about 5,000 Confederates. This left the Confederate commander, General Beauregard, with about 2,500 men to man the Petersburg defenses.

The weakening of the Bermuda Hundred defenses, Smith's excess caution, and Hancock's disability had allowed the Confederates to survive the first day of the siege at Petersburg. Lee's army, and the relative security it would bring, had not yet arrived, though.

The Union had another opportunity to take the city the next day, on June 16, 1864. General Ambrose Burnside and his IX Corps arrived, giving the Union substantially more men in the Petersburg area than the Confederates had. The Union attacks, however, were carried out with little vigor, and they accomplished nothing. A large chunk of Confederate trenches was taken by Union troops on June 17. Once again, though, this success was not followed up. The Army of the Potomac had long had problems with moving quickly and coordinating attacks. General-in-Chief Grant had not yet managed to change these bad habits.

The next day, Saturday, June 18, the Union tried again, making an early morning attack. The troops hit nothing but empty trenches. Beauregard had pulled back, and it would take the Union forces some time to find his new positions.

Most of the Army of the Potomac was now on the scene. Lee's army was starting to arrive, since Lee had finally recognized that Petersburg was indeed Grant's main target. Despite these reinforcements, the Union troops still greatly outnumbered their enemy. George Meade, the commander of the Army of the Potomac and Grant's immediate subordinate, tried to plan a major attack to take place at noon.

Bad News From the War Front

Battle P Field in
front of Petersburg VA
June 26th 1864

Mrs Forsyth

Ere this I presume you have heard of the Death of your Husband while gallantly defending the flag. We were ordered to Charge the enemy on Friday the 17th of June* your Husband went in the charge with us* it was a very warm day and the Hot Sun was more than he was able to withstand* we were ordered to the foot of a hill to rest* your husband Mr William Powell and several other of our Company were Sitting under a tree and conversing on the Subject of the Charge I cannot Say whether it was a grape Shot of a piece of Shell that come from the enemys gun* it Struck Mr Powell first taking off his entire head above the lower jaw and passed on to Mr Forsyth* it went under the lower jaw and come out of his mouth killing him instantly

I saw him buried and it was done as well as we could do it under the circumstances* we wrapped his blanket around him and now he fills a Patriots Grave* he was very much esteemed by all who knew him was always ready and willing to do his duty as a Soldier and Patriot* I believe I have given the particulars as near as I am able* I will return the likeness of Mr Forsyth with the next mail* yours with Respect

Sargeant William Hasson
Company F 37th Wis Vol.

The American Civil War can be called the first major "electronic war." The telegraph allowed for communication between distant points in hours rather than days or weeks. A group of Union signalmen are shown here at a temporary telegraph station.

He even went so far as to send his corps commanders instructions to telegraph his headquarters to find out the exact time, so the attacks would be simultaneous. This early effort at "synchronizing watches" was not successful. A modern historian explained, "Somewhere in the strained machinery of the army, a gear wheel went askew, the various pieces of the Army of the Potomac and the Army of the James lurched piecemeal into battle, with Meade helpless to affect the course of events." The individual attacks failed, resulting in heavy Union casualties.

Some assaults were not even made. Some units of the II Corps refused to attack late on June 18. This was a very strange action. Units were far more likely to panic once they got into combat than to refuse to enter combat at all.

Some later observers blamed this unusual refusal to fight on the lingering effects of the slaughter the II Corps had suffered in their unsuccessful attack at Cold Harbor with Smith's XVIII corps several weeks before. More likely, the unit's reluctance came from the last three days spent at Petersburg, as they saw how their efforts and lives were wasted by poor leadership. The men had developed a sense of strategy as good as that of their commanders, particularly since many of the experienced officers had fallen as casualties during the previous two months. The troops knew what would work and what would not. Perhaps more important, the men were exhausted from 40 days of near-constant marching or fighting since the start of General Grant's spring campaign. Despite this incident, the II Corps performed well in most of its remaining battles. Grant, however, would spend the next ten months trying to fully coordinate the various elements of the Army of the Potomac.

By the end of Saturday, June 18, more troops from the Army of Northern Virginia have arrived. The chance for a quick and easy Union victory was over. That same day, Hancock temporarily turned over command of the II Corps to his senior division commander, Major General David Burney, and went on medical leave.

On June 21, Butler accused Smith of being excessively slow in the attack on Petersburg, implying that he might lose his command. Smith responded sharply to Butler that he was not scared of the threat. In fact, Smith wrote letters to Grant and asked to be relieved from duty with the Army of the James. Grant first considered having Smith sent to the Midwest. Then, Grant decided to put Smith in active command of all Butler's troops, leaving Butler as just administrative head of his department. Smith then took a ten-day leave. Before he left, he stopped by to see Grant and to criticize Meade's command of the Army of the Potomac. When Smith returned, he was in for a shock. Butler had been returned to active command of the Army of the James. Smith had been assigned to New York to await further orders. These orders never came.

Smith later declared that Butler had blackmailed Grant by threatening to reveal that Grant was drinking heavily. Rumors had accused Grant of having an alcohol problem. Butler denied the charge. Grant ignored it entirely. It was most likely Smith's poor performance at Petersburg that convinced Grant it was not worth tolerating Smith's frequent criticism of his colleagues. Butler may have been a barely competent general, but he had more political power than Smith, and he was easier to get along with. For the time being, Butler kept his job.

Even as these political and personal battles raged, the war was continuing. Back at Petersburg and at Richmond 20 miles (32 kilometers) away, the siege had begun.

President Abraham Lincoln, at 6 feet 4 inches, was substantially taller than most of his contemporaries. He is shown in this 1862 photograph with General George McClellan (far left). McClellan was one of Ulysses S. Grant's unsuccessful predecessors as general-in-chief, commanding general of all armies of the United States.

Getting to Petersburg

It is impossible to conceive a field worse adapted to the movements of a grand army. . . . The whole face of the country is thickly wooded, with only an occasional opening, and intersected by a few narrow wood-roads. . . . It was a region of gloom and the shadow of death.

—Reverend Theodore Irving, 1873

The siege of Petersburg began three years and two months after the Confederates had fired on Fort Sumter in Charleston Harbor, South Carolina, and touched off the Civil War. Seven Southern states had refused to accept Abraham Lincoln's November 1860 election as president. They saw Lincoln as a danger to their way of life, which was based on slavery. These states left the Union between December 1860 and March 1861, and set up the Confederate States of America. Four other Southern states, including Virginia, left the Union after the firing on Fort Sumter, refusing to comply with Lincoln's request for troops to crush the Southern rebellion.

The Civil War had started well for the Confederates in Virginia. They won the first major battle of the war, the First Battle of Bull Run, fought near Manassas, Virginia, in July 1861. In March 1862, however, Union General George McClellan, commanding what was now the Union Army of the Potomac, moved his troops by sea from northern Virginia to Hampton. They marched up the peninsula between the James and York rivers, until they were within six miles (10 kilometers) of Richmond.

The Union forces might have taken the city, if not for the efforts of Confederate Major General John B. Magruder at Yorktown. Magruder bluffed McClellan into thinking the Confederate force of about 10,000 men was at least equal to McClellan's 100,000 troops. McClellan was always inclined to greatly overestimate enemy strength. Magruder played on McClellan's chronic caution and overestimation with tricks, such as marching the same units through clearings, visible to Union observers, several times. Empty trains ran back and forth to just behind Confederate lines, out of sight but close enough to be heard. Campfires were lit at night to further convey the image of a large army. These tricks gave the main Confederate army in Virginia, under General Joseph Johnston, time to get back from Manassas, 75 miles (121 kilometers) to the north.

Deception has its place, as does strategic withdrawal. However, the Union was able to come within six miles (10 kilometers) of Richmond. Johnston, a very cautious commander and one who was actually outnumbered, had to fight. His army attacked the Union troops on May 31, 1862, at the Battle of Seven Pines. Johnston was badly wounded on the first day of this battle.

After the battle, General Robert E. Lee was given command of Johnston's Confederate army. He immediately renamed it the Army of Northern Virginia. The name reflected the place Lee intended for this army to fight. By the end of June, after a series of battles, the Union troops had been driven back to Fort Monroe, the place from which they had started three months before. At the end of August, both sides were back at Manassas. Lee won the Second Battle of Bull Run in late August, defeating a new Union army under John Pope, the third major Union commander in Virginia. The Union high command in Virginia was becoming a "revolving door" as Lincoln searched for a general who would be able to win.

With the permission of Confederate President Jefferson Davis, Lee decided to follow up his victory at Bull Run with an invasion of the North. On September 3, 1862, Lee began this invasion by crossing the Potomac River into Maryland. Although slavery was legal in Maryland, the state had remained part of the Union.

George McClellan was given back his Union troops and sent after Lee. The Battle of Antietam, which took place on September 17, 1862, was the single bloodiest day of battle or other violence in American history. More than 5,000 men from both armies were killed at Antietam. During the battle, the Confederate army held off a Union army twice its size for 14 hours. Still, the Southerners withdrew back into Virginia two days later, putting an early end to Lee's campaign. The battle was also a turning point for the North, as it gave Lincoln an opportunity to issue the preliminary Emancipation

Proclamation, a first step toward ending slavery in the United States.

McClellan's slow pursuit gave Lee time to move south safely. It also cost McClellan his job. He was replaced by Major General Ambrose Burnside. The new commander lost the Battle of Fredericksburg, Virginia, in December 1862, to an Army of Northern Virginia that had fully recovered from its heavy losses at Antietam. Six weeks later, Lincoln, increasingly frustrated with his commanding generals' failures, replaced Burnside with Joseph Hooker. Lincoln still had not found the right general, however. Hooker lost the Battle of Chancellorsville, Virginia, in May 1863.

Lee invaded the North again in June 1863. This campaign ended with his defeat at Gettysburg, Pennsylvania, in July to yet another Northern commander, George Meade. Damaged but still dangerous, the Army of Northern Virginia retreated back to Virginia. Meade had done well in his victory at Gettysburg, but he did not quickly pursue and attack after the battle. Lincoln thought Meade had missed a chance to destroy Lee.

A solution to Lincoln's command problems began to present itself the very day Lee left Gettysburg—July 4, 1863. On that day, Vicksburg, Mississippi, the most important Confederate position on the Mississippi River, surrendered to Union forces under Ulysses S. Grant. In what was called the "West" in the Civil War— Tennessee, Mississippi, Georgia, and Kentucky—the situation for the North was almost opposite what it was in Virginia. Northern commanders in the West were usually better than their counterparts in Virginia. Fighting Confederate armies that were most often inferior to Lee and his troops, the Union generals in the West won most of their battles.

Grant became the most prominent Union commander

in the West, although others who fought there—including William Sherman, George Thomas and Philip Sheridan—became famous later in the war. Grant was caught in a surprise attack at Shiloh, Tennessee, in April 1862, but Union reinforcements and the death of the Southern commander enabled him to reverse the course of the battle.

On September 19–20, 1863, the Confederate Army of Tennessee defeated the Union Army of the Cumberland in a fierce fight at Chickamauga Creek in northern Georgia. The Union army retreated northward, to Chattanooga, Tennessee. The Southern army began to besiege the city, although the Union supply lines were never cut. In mid-November, about two months after the siege began, a substantially reinforced Union army, under Grant's direct command, relieved the siege and dealt a major defeat to the Confederate forces there.

This victory prompted Illinois Congressman Elihu B. Washburne, a friend of Lincoln's and the man who had helped Grant get his first Civil War commission, to introduce a bill in the congress, which was passed, reviving the rank of lieutenant general, which had last been held by George Washington. Grant was formally promoted to this rank on March 2, 1864. He was appointed general-in-chief of the Union army ten days later.

President Abraham Lincoln knew he needed a tough commander, someone who would be able to coordinate all the Union armies in both the East and the West. He needed a persistent leader who would grab hold of Lee's army and not let go until the war ended in a Union victory, regardless of how strongly the Confederates fought back. Lincoln hoped Grant was the man he needed.

Grant seemed to be less dynamic and popular than Robert E. Lee was. Grant did not often make a good first impression. After his first meeting with Grant,

Lieutenant-General Ulysses S. Grant, general-in-chief of the United States Army, in a photo probably taken in the fall of 1864 in Washington, D.C.

George Meade wrote to his wife that Grant was "not a striking man, is very reticent, has never mixed with the world, indeed is somewhat ill at ease in the presence of strangers; hence a first impression is never favorable."

Some members of the Army of the Potomac as well as people outside of the army, were worried about Grant, who had a reputation for having a drinking problem. Although the rumor caused some concern, drinking was not really held against a general in the Army of the Potomac. As a later historian pointed out, referring to a theoretical general, not to anyone in particular, "A general who never got drunk was a rarity—so much so that his sobriety was always mentioned in his biography, as a sign that he stood above the common run." There is little evidence that Grant actually had a drinking problem at this time. More officers and men were more worried about the fact that Grant had been fighting in the western theater of the war. The last general to come from the West, John Pope, had not performed well at all. Grant had also never faced Confederate generals as talented as Robert E. Lee, the best leader the Confederates had.

Others, however, knew what to expect from Grant. James Longstreet, Lee's senior corps commander, warned his men not to underestimate Grant. An old friend of Grant's, Longstreet pointed out that Grant had the persistence Meade lacked. He said, "That man [Grant] will fight us every day and every hour until the end of the war."

Grant determined that the final campaigns of the Civil War should take a different approach than that used in the previous three years. No more would there be long periods of inaction with only an occasional major battle. One of the best summaries of Grant's plans, and the situation he faced on taking over the Union army, is a quotation from his own report on the last year of the war, which he submitted after the war had ended:

> From an early period in the rebellion I had been impressed with the idea that active and continuous operations of all the troops that could be brought into the field, regardless of season and weather, were necessary to a speedy termination of the war. . . .
>
> The armies in the East and West acted independently and without concert, like a balky team, no two ever pulling together, enabling the enemy to use to great advantage his interior lines of communication for transporting troops from east to west, re-enforcing the army most vigorously pressed, and to furlough large numbers, during seasons of inactivity on our part, to go to their homes and do the work of producing for the support of their armies. It was a question whether our numerical strength and resources were not more than balanced by these disadvantages and the enemy's . . . position. . . .
>
> [I determined] first, to use the greatest number of troops practicable against the armed force of the enemy, preventing him from using the same force at different seasons against first one and then another of our armies, and the possibility of repose for refitting and producing necessary supplies for carrying on resistance; second, to hammer continuously against the armed force of the enemy and his resources, until by mere attrition, if in no other way, [the Union would win the Civil War.]

On May 4, 1864, the Army of the Potomac began to advance southward into the heavily forested area of northern Virginia known as the Wilderness, about 10 miles (16 kilometers) west of Fredericksburg. Grant's

On May 4, 1864, the Union army began to cross the Rapidan River, in Virginia, and enter the area known as the Wilderness. The continuous series of campaigns, which would not end until Appomattox, had begun. This photo shows supply wagons from the Federal VI Corps crossing the Rapidan at a place called Germanna Ford.

plan was to move quickly through the Wilderness, swing west, and attack Lee's army—or at least fight in open country. Grant assumed that Lee would bring his army out of the strong entrenchments near Mine Run, several miles farther west, to avoid being cut off from Richmond and his supplies or having his positions attacked in the rear. The engagement did not quite work out the way Grant had planned it. Lee's army attacked Grant in the Wilderness on May 5—just a few miles from the site of the Battle of Chancellorsville—starting a confused two-day battle.

Visibility in areas of the Wilderness battlefield is still limited today. The region can be shadowy and overcast, even on a sunny day. Back then, the forest and brush were thicker and more tangled than they are today. Heavy smoke from the firing of weapons and from sparks that set brush and leaves on fire—and sometimes burned the wounded to death—limited visibility even more. The layout of the area allowed only occasional use of artillery, a major strength of the Union troops. The battle became a series of separate and confused smaller fights. The two forces fired at and were shot at by an enemy they could not see (and were sometimes accidentally shot by their own troops). Both armies were still in the same place on the evening of May 6.

On May 7, both armies sat, waiting for the other to move. The Union moved that night. Their left, southern edge stayed in place as the right began to move, swinging in back of the army and then moving south to lead the advance. This method was designed to avoid a damaging enemy attack on their flank while they were in motion and least prepared to resist. Ulysses S. Grant, George Meade, and their staffs led the advance down Brock Road. They came to Orange Plank Road. Turning left would take them back to Washington, D.C. On the other hand, they could stay on Brock Road and continue south. The custom of the Army of the Potomac in past battles had been to retreat after each seemingly inevitable defeat.

One of the best descriptions of what happened next comes from Grant's memoirs:

> With my staff and a small escort of cavalry I preceded the troops. Meade and his staff accompanied me. The greatest enthusiasm was manifest as we passed by. No doubt it was inspired by the fact that the movement was south. It indicated to them that they had passed through the "beginning of the end" in the battle just fought.

The "end" would take a long time, however, as Grant's men learned a few days later at Spotsylvania Court House, Virginia.

Lee detected Grant's move south. Rather than try to attack the Union troops who remained in their trenches, Lee ordered his men to head south as well. He guessed that the Union army was headed to Spotsylvania. He was right—and his Confederate units won the race. The Confederates entrenched, and held off the first of a series of Union attacks. Entrenching—the digging of protective trenches that faced the enemy—had become popular during the fall campaigns of 1863, after the Battle of Gettysburg. A modern historian notes that, "In the winter of 1863–1864 soldiers on both sides of the American Civil War learned the value of temporary field entrenchments. It did not result from any articulated shift in tactical doctrine, but rather seems to have emerged out of a spontaneous recognition by veteran troops that to dig was to survive."

Entrenching fit in with the changing realities of the Civil War after Grant took over the Union army. His focus was on the campaign as a whole, rather than on each battle. He believed that, though it would be nice to get Lee to come out to fight one last decisive battle, it was more likely that the Union would have to use attrition to wear down the Confederates to a point where they could no longer resist.

A "war of attrition"—in which the opposing forces pounded away at each other, not in hopes of decisive victory but to try and force the other to run out of men and resources first—would be unwinnable for the South. Lee knew his army was no longer strong enough for the wide-ranging strategic offensives of a year before—despite Confederate General Jubal Early's raid on Washington, D.C., which began a few days before the Petersburg siege. Local offensives, at places called targets of opportunity, remained a Confederate tactic until the end of the war in the East. Lee still had hopes of winning a war of nerves with the North, particularly during the 40 Days Campaign from the Wilderness to Petersburg. If Lee could prevent Grant from winning a major battle, perhaps the people of the North would decide that the war could not be won. They might force the Lincoln administration to make peace, or vote Lincoln out of office in the November 1864 presidential elections. Lee knew he had to act fast. At the start of the 40 Days, he told Major General Jubal Early, "We must destroy this army of Grant's before he gets to James River. If he gets there, it will become a siege, and then it will be a mere question of time."

It would be equally dangerous to the survival of Lee's army if Grant got around the Confederates and cut them off from Richmond and the supply center at Petersburg. Lee needed mobility. That is why he feared that a siege might take place. His army needed supplies to have any hope of continuing the war, which is why he had to protect Richmond and Petersburg.

After the Battle of the Wilderness, whenever they were not engaged in a local attack, Lee's men stayed in their trenches. Union forces, remaining within firing

Grant and his staff in conference at Grant's temporary headquarters, Massaponax Church, Virginia, May 21, 1864. Grant is bending over the bench, actually a church pew, to the left of the picture, to look at a map. George Meade, commander of the Army of the Potomac, is just to Grant's left mostly blocked by Grant. Charles A. Dana, Assistant Secretary of War, is sitting just to the right and in front of the two trees.

range of the Confederates, had to dig and occupy their own trenches. Soldiers on both sides learned that trenches could only rarely be taken by a direct frontal attack, and then only if the attackers were particularly skilled. At Spotsylvania, on May 10 and May 12, the Union nearly pulled off such frontal attacks. In both cases, they aimed at a bulge in the Confederate lines called the "Mule Shoe." The attacking units stormed the trenches without taking time to fire. This meant they spent far less time exposed to enemy fire. The Union forces did not use enough men in the first attack to defeat the Confederates, though. Heavy forces were used for the second effort, however, two days later. Again, the Union failed to take the trenches, as the Confederates held off the attackers long enough to build a second trench line at the base of the Mule Shoe.

From Spotsylvania, Grant sent a telegram to Lincoln and Secretary of War Edwin Stanton. It stated that he would fight it out even if it took all summer. The persistent Grant was willing to keep pressing Lee to battle, when this was the best strategy. By May 20, however, Grant ordered another move south, in an attempt to outflank Lee. Inconclusive fighting took place at Hanover Junction and the North Anna River a few days later. By May 30, the Union army had moved to a point known as Cold Harbor (a term for an inn where shelter was available but not hot food).

The Cold Harbor attack was delayed from June 2 to June 3, since not all the Union forces had arrived in the area yet. This gave the Confederates extra time to get ready. The Confederate positions looked weaker than they actually were. In a battle that lasted less than half an hour, the Union lost roughly 2,000 dead and 5,000 wounded. Considering the brief time spent in actual fighting, the 7,000 Union and 1,500 Confederate casualties made Cold Harbor the bloodiest period of fighting in the Civil War.

After Cold Harbor, Grant was four miles (6.5 kilometers) from Richmond, but stalemated by seemingly impregnable Confederate positions. The armies had been in continuous contact for almost a month. Despite his reputation as a "butcher" who was unconcerned about casualties, Grant was a very flexible commander. In fact, Lee actually lost a higher percentage of his men in battle than Grant. Instead of making a direct strike at Richmond, he decided to cut off the supply lines to both the Confederate capital and Lee's army. This could be done by moving south about 24 miles (39 kilometers) and taking the town of Petersburg, which controlled all but one of the rail lines into Richmond.

The First Month

Petersburg trenches, with rows of sharpened wooden stakes, called *chevaux-de-frise*. These were designed to slow down or stop attacking infantry.

I have seen your dispatch expressing your unwillingness to
break your hold where you are. Neither am I willing.
Hold on with a bulldog grip, and chew and choke as much as possible.

—Abraham Lincoln to Ulysses S. Grant, August 17, 1864

The Union's initial attempts to take Petersburg by storm failed. Lee's army had already arrived. Grant, hoping for a quick victory but, at the same time, planning for a long stay, issued his first major order of the siege. The troops of his two armies in the area, the Army of the Potomac and the Army of the James, were told to dig "permanent" entrenchments. Even before his command, the Union soldiers were already digging in. They had learned the lessons of the Wilderness, Spotsylvania Court House, and Cold Harbor.

Stronger trenches would protect the men from the inevitable local attacks by Lee's army. They would also enable fewer men to hold the Union lines. Units could be pulled out of line and used as a mobile strike force to try to break through what appeared to be weak spots in Lee's line. The Union troops would also try to move around the ends of the Confederate position and turn the flanks, to bring on the still-desired decisive battle.

Considering the skill of their opponents, such a battle was unlikely for the North. For the time being, then, a strong trench system would enable the Union to keep extending the lines to the north and south. Lee would be pressured to do the same, and he had fewer men to use. Eventually, if the Union lines stretched far enough, Lee would not have enough men to respond.

Robert E. Lee wrote to Confederate President Jefferson Davis on June 19, 1864, to bring him up to date on the military situation. Lee considered Petersburg the key point of his defenses, and he knew it was there that Grant would concentrate his efforts. Lee was moving troops from the immediate area of Richmond to Petersburg. This strategy would seem to leave the Confederate capital insufficiently protected. However, Lee assured Davis that, if he received early word of a Union thrust at Richmond, and if the railroad and roads connecting the two cities were kept open and in good repair, he could get enough troops to Richmond in time to save the city. Grant and Meade, for the moment, were focusing their efforts elsewhere.

From north to south, the Union troops in the Petersburg-Richmond front consisted of the XVIII Corps (part of it north of the Appomattox River), the VI Corps, the II Corps, the IX Corps, and the V Corps. Grant's first move was to pull the II Corps out of line so it could be used as a maneuver force. The VI and IX Corps were ordered to extend to take up the front formerly held by the II Corps. Grant then added the VI Corps to the strike force, ordering the XVIII Corps front extended to the south. The II Corps was first ordered to a spot to the left rear of the Union lines. About 5:00 A.M. on June 21, the corps was told to take a position on the left of the Union lines, at Jerusalem Plank Road, and link with the V Corps. The VI Corps was ordered to move to the left of the II Corps. Despite the short distance the II Corps had to travel, the move took all day, since the roads available were limited. The Union cavalry was preparing for a supporting raid, and was not on hand to scout out the best roads for the Union advance or to identify exact enemy positions.

On June 21, while the II and VI Corps were getting into position, Grant had the distraction of an unannounced visit from President Lincoln. At Grant's suggestion, they rode out to visit the VI Corps, still part of the main Petersburg lines. At VI Corps headquarters, joined by General Meade, Grant and Lincoln went over maps of the coming move.

That evening, the II corps finished its move into position along the Jerusalem Plank Road, on the left flank of the V Corps. The II Corps division under Brigadier General Francis Barlow advanced all the way to the Weldon Railroad, itself a major Union target. However, the division lost contact with the rest of the corps, however, and was called back. By early on the morning of June 22, the VI Corps had moved into position on the left of the II Corps, on the far left of the Union lines.

That day, June 22, Union plans called for the VI Corps to advance about two miles (three kilometers) to the west, toward the Weldon Railroad. Once the corps reached the railroad, it would turn right, to the north, and attack in the direction of Petersburg. The II Corps would guard the VI Corps's right flank, while keeping in contact with the V Corps and the rest of the Union line. The movement would resemble a door closing, with the II Corps as the hinge. While this operation was under way, a large Union cavalry force, under James Wilson, would be cutting the Weldon Railroad farther to the south of Petersburg. The movement would end with the Union closely encircling almost three-quarters of Petersburg.

This seemed like a good plan. However, there could be problems. The topography of the area—the "design" of the ground, particularly how flat the ground was and how heavily wooded the area—would make it harder than the Union commanders thought for the II Corps to remain in contact with the V Corps on its right flank. The terrain was heavily wooded, making it very difficult for units moving through the woods to even see, let alone remain near, men moving in the road. There was only one road in the area running east–west outside of the Confederate lines. Even worse, this road did not run directly towards the Confederate lines, but diverged towards the northwest. If a gap developed in the Union lines, particularly on the II Corps area, the "hinge" of the advance, it would provide an opening and an invitation for a Confederate attack.

When the Union advance began, at 8:00 A.M., the units had trouble staying in line. Barlow's division of the II Corps was ordered to maintain contact with the rest of the II Corps. As a result, a gap developed between the II Corps and the VI Corps to its left.

The Union troops were not very familiar with the area, despite the brief advance they had made over the same ground the day before. Unfortunately for them, Brigadier General William "Billy" Mahone, who was ordered by Lee to take his division and attack the Union advance, did know the area. Mahone had been a railroad engineer there before the war. He knew that there was a deep ravine nearby. When he learned of the developing gap in the

Union soldiers dig earthworks near Warren Station, on the military railroad between the Union supply base at City Point and the Union lines. The Union soldiers had established this railroad to bring supplies very close to where they were actually needed.

Union lines, Mahone realized that the ravine would allow him to attack the II Corps on its left. Another Confederate division would be sent to divert the VI Corps and keep it from coming to the aid of the II Corps.

Not long before 3:00 P.M. that afternoon, June 22, a Union major named Moncena Dunn, of the 18th Massachusetts Infantry, awoke from a bad dream. Dunn reported the dream to some of his fellow officers. He had dreamed that the Confederates attacked the Union lines in their rear and captured the entire regiment. The other officers

William Mahone

The name William Mahone appears frequently in stories about the siege of Petersburg. He is not as well known as many of Robert E. Lee's other subordinate generals, but Mahone was probably Lee's most effective division commander during the last year of the war. Mahone was not an impressive man to look at. He was short and very skinny. He habitually wore a civilian-style coat with his insignia on the collar, and a wide-brimmed hat. He also had a high-pitched voice. Mahone, who had stomach trouble, ate only milk and eggs. He even kept a cow and chickens near his tent. Despite these quirks, as a military leader, it was said that when Mahone moved, someone among the enemy was sure to be hurt.

Mahone was born in 1826, and attended the Virginia Military Institute (VMI). Mahone worked primarily as a railroad engineer and a railroad president before the Civil War. He spent much time surveying areas near Petersburg, which gave him valuable familiarity with the region.

When the war started, Mahone was a brigadier general of the Virginia militia. In April 1861, Mahone and his men played a role in tricking the Union into withdrawing from the Gosport Navy Yard in Portsmouth—beginning what seemed to become a Confederate tradition in that area. Mahone had his men across the river in Norfolk cheer as empty trains pulled in and out. The Union commander became convinced that heavy Confederate reinforcements were arriving and withdrew from the Navy Yard.

Mahone was promoted to brigadier general and given command of a brigade in November 1861. Mahone and his brigade performed well in most of the battles of the Army of Northern Virginia, though they had little part in the Battle of Gettysburg. On May 6, 1864, at the Battle of the Wilderness, Mahone took over Richard Anderson's division when Anderson took over command of the 1st Corps.

Mahone found his true calling as a division commander. His best moment came during the Battle of the Crater. Told to send reinforcements to the endangered front, Mahone led his men personally. He succeeded in restoring the breach, then played the major role in blunting a serious Union threat.

Mahone returned to engineering after the Civil War ended. In the late 1870s, he entered Virginia politics as a Democrat. In 1881, the Virginia legislature elected Mahone to the U.S. Senate. Best described as a political moderate, Mahone was willing to work with Republicans, and even with former slaves. The Democrats regained power in the mid- to late 1880s. Mahone was not reelected. Mahone died in 1895, and is buried in Petersburg.

laughed. They thought there was little chance that Dunn's dream could come true.

At 3:00 P.M., however, the two divisions to the immediate left of the one in which Dunn served had been in their new positions for less than an hour. Their movement had created a gap with the VI Corps. General Barlow, commanding the division furtherst to the left, tried to secure his position by moving two brigades back at almost a right angle to the rest of the line. Soon after this move, but before the Union had finished entrenching, a Confederate brigade attacked, giving the high-pitched "rebel yell" that had become all too familiar to the Union troops. The thick woods prevented the Confederates from attacking in a single line. Part of the assaulting brigade came out of the woods first and took heavy fire from the Union troops. This brigade temporarily withdrew back into the woods. A supporting brigade was then brought up and the attack began again.

The brief first attack had given Barlow enough warning to send some reinforcements to his left. These delayed, but did not stop, Mahone's fierce attack. One of Barlow's brigades was able to withdraw to the Union positions built the day before. Many individual Union soldiers, when they realized they could not resist the Confederate attack, ran to the same positions. These areas served as a rallying point for the II Corps.

The shock of the Confederate attack spread to the next Union division, just to the east. This division was effectively routed, as the flank and rear of John Gibbon's division, the next in line, were uncovered. The Confederates hit the rear. This division's men first saw panicky troops from the two other divisions, yelling at them to fall back. As Major General Andrew A. Humphreys, then chief of staff of the Army of the Potomac, later wrote, "So unexpected was this attack on Gibbon's left, that the greater part of several regiments were captured with their colors." The small

15th Massachusetts Infantry did not fall back in time, and virtually all of its members were captured. The same happened to the 19th Massachusetts, whose Major Dunn had predicted the defeat and capture in his dream just a few hours earlier.

The Confederates enjoyed great success for about an hour, when the attack quickly came to an end. This very success actually worked against the Confederates, who had to escort captured Union prisoners to the Confederate rear lines, losing some Confederate fighting troops. At the same time, II Corps was inflicting as well as taking casualties. It was also able to fall back to stronger positions that had been built the day before. Finally, the Confederate division told to support Mahone was delayed in coming to Mahone's support. The commander had been having trouble controlling his division in the heavy woods. He was also worried that the Union VI Corps would advance and over-whelm his division.

He need not have worried. The VI Corps did nothing for most of the day. An advance finally began at 7:00 P.M., but it soon faltered because of the thick woods and the oncoming darkness.

On the morning of June 23, Grant reported to Washington, D.C., that the Confederate attack had caused few problems. The next day, he had to change his evalua-tion, writing to General Halleck that "The affair was a stampede and surprise to both parties and ought to have been turned in our favor."

Union efforts in this area continued. The II Corps was sent back to try to retake its lines of June 22. This was done with no opposition, since Mahone had withdrawn back to the main Confederate lines the day before. The VI Corps was also ordered to advance, but it encountered some Confederate resistance and failed to make any progress. Mahone's men chased away members of the Union VI Corps attempting to

Wrecked railroad depot in Richmond, Virginia. This photo was taken not long after the fall of Richmond in April 1865.

destroy part of the Weldon railroad. The Union destroyed only about half a mile (about one kilometer) of track, and most of two Union regiments were captured.

Despite this loss, the Union had another major operation under way at that time. James Wilson and August Kautz were leading a cavalry raid. Grant had ordered a wide sweep to the south, around the Confederate right. The bulk of cavalry from both sides was away to the west, and Grant expected that only one Confederate cavalry division, under General William Henry Fitzhugh "Rooney" Lee, might possibly offer resistance.

James Wilson, overall commander of the raid, left early on the morning of June 22 with 5,000 men. By mid-morning, his troops reached Ream's Station on the Weldon Railroad, about 10 miles (16 kilometers) south of Petersburg. The Union cavalry burned the railroad buildings, tore up tracks, and then continued west toward Dinwiddie Court House. By nightfall, the Union cavalry had reached Ford's Station on the Southside rail line, headed west from Petersburg. They took a greater haul this time. They found two fully loaded Confederate supply trains, which they burned. They also destroyed station buildings. Here, the Union cavalry used an effective, but time-consuming, method of destroying rails. They heated the rails in fires made from rail ties until they were red-hot. The rails were then bent out of shape, which made them useless as replacement rails to repair the lines. The cavalry's busy day ended when they made camp just before midnight, 50 miles (81 kilometers) from their starting point.

Kautz's division led the advance from Ford's Station the next day, headed toward another rail line. Wilson's division followed at a more leisurely pace. Rooney Lee's Confederate division was catching up, however, so the Union cavalry had only enough time to overturn rails, which was annoying to the Confederates but easy to fix. The Union divisions met up at Burke's Station, where Kautz's men had already destroyed all the buildings. The cavalry then headed southwest. Thirty miles (48 kilometers) away, Kautz and his division reached the Staunton River and its bridge. By this time, though, the Union forces no longer had the advantage of taking the Confederates by surprise. A thousand members of the Virginia home guard defended the bridge and drove Kautz off. With Rooney Lee still pressing Wilson, the general decided it was time to head back.

The return trip would be much more difficult than Wilson expected. On June 28, the Union reached Stoney Creek Depot. The Confederates, who still held the Weldon Railroad, were now between Wilson's cavalry and the safety of the Union lines. Even more unexpectedly, Wilson and his men ran into Major General Wade Hampton with his two Southern cavalry divisions. Unable to break through after a day of combat, Wilson ordered Kautz to take his division, circle the Confederate cavalry, and head to Ream's Station, where they should be safe.

Instead of safety, however, Kautz found more Confederate cavalry and infantry waiting for him at Ream's Station. Wilson joined Kautz the next day, but found that Kautz's forces were surrounded by Confederates on three sides. The Union had no choice but to burn their own wagons, destroy their cannons, and head southwest. When the Confederates attacked, Kautz and his division were unable to escape. They became separated from Wilson. Kautz sent his men into a swamp situated on the Confederates' left flank. His men were able to get through with no opposition, and seven hours later, they rode, exhausted, back to Union lines at Petersburg.

Confederates chased Wilson's division 20 miles (32 kilometers) south, farther away from Union lines. Wilson and his troops finally managed to cross a river, then swing north to safety.

The Union cavalry raid had mixed results. Wilson had lost all of his artillery and one-quarter of his force. He had managed to harm the Confederate store of supplies, and to close two major railroads for nine weeks. In his report about the last year of the war, Grant later wrote, "The damage to the enemy in this expedition more than compensated for the losses we sustained. It severed all connection by railroad with Richmond for several weeks."

The raid was a turning point of another kind, too. The Wilson-Kautz raid did not accomplish all it had intended. However, unlike two years earlier, the Union troops were the ones taking action, and the Confederates were the ones responding. Grant had by no means won the war. Still, Lee had lost a major engagement and would never regain the strategic initiative. The war had become Grant's to win or lose.

Digging
a Mine

Union Soldiers from Battery B, First Pennsylvania Light Artillery, in the lines during the siege of Petersburg, July 30, 1864. This photo was taken by an assistant to famed Civil War photographer, Matthew Brady. Many "Brady" photographs were actually taken by his assistants.

We could blow that damned fort out of existence
if we could run a mine shaft under it.

—Soldier in 48th Pennsylvania Volunteer Infantry, June 1864

The next few weeks were quiet, as much as the front around Petersburg was ever quiet. Men were still being killed and wounded. However, the major focus of action had shifted to the Shenandoah Valley, and to Washington, D.C. Three years into the war and several months into what the North hoped would be the conflict's final campaign, the Confederate force that showed up on July 12 at the gates of the capital city made quite an impression. On July 12–13, even President Lincoln left for Fort Stevens to the north, to stand on the parapets and watch the fighting. One Union officer, believed to be Oliver Wendell Holmes, Jr. (a captain from Massachusetts who later became a justice of the U.S. Supreme Court) grew so concerned about Lincoln's safety that he yelled, "Get down, you fool."

Fortunately for the North, the Union VI Corps, already on the way, showed up July 13th and forced the Confederates to withdraw back toward the Shenandoah Valley. The VI Corps slowly pursued the Confederate troops, which were under the command of Jubal Early.

Jubal Early's raid and the Shenandoah Valley campaign that followed shifted the focus of attention, at least briefly, away from Petersburg and Richmond. Even so, an interesting move was under way at Petersburg at the same time. This operation would become the central event of the Petersburg siege. Of the many and varied plans being made, this one was unusual, since it emerged from the remark of a bored Union soldier.

The siege of Petersburg was not a static battle, with both sides shooting each other from the relative safety of their entrenchments. Rather, it included a series of moves and offensives, usually but not always initiated by the Union. The war in the East was no longer a war of movement. When a Union advance was over, having met a certain goal or been forced back by Lee, the Union troops returned to their increasingly elaborate trench system. The Confederates did the same.

Lee had probably been right when he said that, once a siege began, it was just a matter of time before the South lost the war. Despite the lack of dramatic success, the Union was slowly stretching its trench system on both flanks, which made the Confederates strain themselves to keep up. Despite their efforts, the Union forces could not be sure how the siege would end. With a presidential election coming up in a few months, Grant did not know if he would have time to see the siege through. Northern voters might end the war by voting out the Lincoln administration and electing a candidate who pledged to negotiate an immediate

Jubal's Raid

On June 12, 1864, Robert E. Lee anticipated that Ulysses S. Grant might take his army and move toward Petersburg, but he could not guess when. Lee realized that something had to done to relieve enemy pressure, secure Virginia's Shenandoah Valley as a source of food, and perhaps even find a way to contribute to Lincoln's defeat in the November presidential election. Lee's idea was to send troops to the Shenandoah Valley to clear the area of Union troops. Jubal Early was chosen to take the 2nd Corps into the valley. If the mission went well and Early successfully cleared the valley of Union troops, he was to head north across the Potomac. He was even authorized to attempt an attack on Washington, D.C.

On July 4, 1864, after they had chased all the Union soldiers out of the Shenandoah Valley, Early's forces crossed the Potomac into Maryland. Major General Lewis Wallace, a political general who later wrote the novel *Ben Hur*, was the Union commander of the district of Maryland. Until reinforcements could arrive, Wallace commanded the only Union troops that stood between Early and Washington. These 6,000 men had to stop 12,000 Confederates.

On the evening of July 9, 1864, Lincoln received a telegram reporting Wallace's defeat, in a battle starting that morning, at the Battle of the Monocacy. The battle ended late in the afternoon, and Early felt it was too late for his men to continue the march to Washington. They would start the next morning. Had there been no battle, Early's men would have arrived at Washington a day before Union reinforcements (already on the way), and might have been able to enter the city.

The fortifications protecting Washington during the Civil War were the most powerful the world had seen. Fort Stevens was the key to the system

Jubal's Raid (continued)

in the north. It protected the Seventh Street Pike, now Georgia Avenue. The problem was that the fortifications were not properly manned. Most of the trained gunners who used to be stationed in the forts had been sent to join the Army of the Potomac in its spring campaign. The troops available were any that could be scraped together—including short-term recruits, invalids, and War Department clerks. Experienced combat troops were on the way, but might not arrive on time.

On July 11, the Confederates began to arrive at Fort Stevens, which is actually inside what is now Washington, D.C., but was then on the outskirts. That same day, Lincoln rode to Fort Stevens to catch a glimpse of the fighting. As Lincoln stood watching the first day's skirmishing, a young Union officer was killed not far from where he was standing.

The VI Corps from the Army of the Potomac started to arrive that same afternoon. By the next day, the corps was fully deployed in and around Fort Stevens. President Lincoln again came to watch the battle, and again stood looking over the wall. Major General Horatio Wright, commanding the VI Corps and the ranking general at Fort Stevens, several times had to ask Lincoln to sit down. Wright finally had to threaten to have Lincoln arrested and removed by a squad of soldiers. Lincoln, amused by Wright's boldness, finally sat with his back to the battlement, but distressed Wright with his habit of getting up every few minutes to take a look at the fighting.

On the second day of skirmishing, Early realized that his men were facing experienced troops, not clerks. He broke off the engagement that afternoon after a limited Union attack, when he saw that the risks were too great. That night, the Confederates withdrew back to the Shenandoah Valley.

peace. As the Union probed the enemy lines, Grant looked for any Confederate weaknesses that might help bring the siege to a speedy conclusion.

The men in the trenches were more concerned with immediate survival than long-term strategy. The men dug. They endured the intense heat, the dry dust from lack of rain, and the increasingly deadly artillery fire, combined with day-to-day boredom when offensives were not under way. Both sides had started to use mortars, artillery pieces with high trajectories that could drop shells almost directly into the trenches. The men responded to the mortars with what were then called "bombproofs." These were early bomb shelters, areas of the trenches with roofs designed to shield the occupant from artillery fire from above as well as artillery fire and gunfire from the front.

Some Union troops thought they found a way to break the stalemate. They were coal miners from Pennsylvania, men who had dug for a living before the war. They were part of the 48th Pennsylvania Infantry Regiment, Robert Potter's division, of Ambrose Burnside's IX Corps. They were virtually at the center of the Union line, farther ahead than the units on either side, at the top of a slope, about 130 yards (119 meters) from the Confederates.

The Confederates stationed at what came to be called "Elliott's Salient" after the commander of the South Carolina brigade defending the area, were in a strategic location. (A salient is an outward-facing bulge in a military defensive line.) Five hundred yards (457 meters) in back of the Confederates ran the Jerusalem Plank Road, the target of several Union thrusts elsewhere on the line. This road ran directly into Petersburg. It was a route for bringing in supplies by wagon—a backup system to help the Confederates compensate for increasing damage to their railroads. Half a mile (about one kilometer) to the northwest, Cemetery Hill dominated Petersburg. Some Union soldiers believed that breaking through here would give them a good chance of capturing Petersburg and splitting the Confederates. If this offensive could be followed up quickly, the fighting in the East might come to an end.

One afternoon, as he stared across at the Confederate positions of Elliott's Salient, one Union soldier commented to his neighbors, "We could blow that damned fort out of existence if we could run a mine shaft under it." Regimental commander Lieutenant Colonel Henry Pleasants, who had been a mining engineer before the war, was passing by at the time and heard the soldier's remark. Pleasants liked the idea. After carefully studying the Confederate position, he went to see his division commander, Brigadier General Robert B. Potter. Potter then went to Burnside with the idea.

Many historians consider Ambrose Burnside one of the worst generals ever. At Antietam in September 1862, it may have been his delays that cost the Union a clear victory. His lack of tactical imagination at Fredericksburg three months later led the Army of the Potomac into its worst defeat in a major battle in the entire Civil War. Burnside was open to innovative ideas, however. When Pleasants approached him, he asked for further details, then approved the project and promised to obtain support from Meade and Grant. Pleasants's men began work on a mine shaft on June 25, 1864.

Meade and Grant were not as enthusiastic as Burnside. In fact, Grant thought the project was being undertaken simply to give the men something to do. A year before, at the siege of Vicksburg, Mississippi, he and William Sherman had their men dig a canal across the narrow strip of land formed by a loop in the Mississippi River, in an attempt to divert the river from Vicksburg and destroy the strategic value of the town. The plan had failed. Ironically, about 20 years later, the river actually did change course to follow the canal.

According to the account later written by his chief of staff at the time, General Andrew A. Humphreys, Meade "assented" to the mining, not exactly an enthusiastic endorsement. Humphreys went on to write that,

> The ground on our side was favorable to running the gallery of the mine [digging the main shaft] screened from observation, but the position was not in other respects suitable . . . the salient itself, as well as all the ground between it and Burnside's advanced line of entrenchments, being exposed to a flank fire on the right and left.

J. C. Duane, chief engineer of the Army of the Potomac, later told a court of inquiry that "the mine as a means of assault . . . is a very unusual way of attacking field fortifications. I do not think that there was any reasonable chance of success by such an attack."

The Union high command almost seemed determined to make their doubts a self-fulfilling prophecy by not supporting the actions needed for the mining effort to work. Despite Burnside's promise, Pleasants received little help. The men had to forage for their own lumber to support the mine shaft. They took what they could from abandoned sawmills and even tore down a bridge. The troops made their own wheelbarrows from cracker boxes with handles. Pleasants was unable to get a surveying instrument he needed to determine how far to dig the mine so it would be right under the Confederate position. He managed to obtain a more primitive device than he wanted, but was at least able to take the measurements.

The mining effort had a major technical problem—supplying breathable air to the men. Breathing, especially for a person working hard, would become more and more difficult as the tunnel got longer. Ventilation problems were the major reasons miners rarely tried to dig tunnels of this length—over 500 feet (152 meters).

Members of the 48th Pennsylvania, mostly coal miners before the war, dig a shaft under Confederate positions. Their intent is to blow up Confederate positions with gunpowder, punching a hole into which Union troops can attack.

Pleasants found a solution. One hundred feet (31 meters) into the shaft, still behind Union lines and shielded from Confederate view by the terrain, a vertical shaft was dug to the surface. An airtight door was placed in the main tunnel, between the shaft and the tunnel opening. The men were then told to build an eight-inch-square (20-centimeter-square) duct, from where they were digging back to under the door. A large fire was kept burning under the vertical shaft. The air heated by the fire headed up the shaft and also sucked in fresh air from the outside. The system would work as the main shaft was dug, and as the men dug two smaller shafts running under the Confederate positions at the end.

The Union high command doubted that the project would work. Most Confederate commanders refused to seriously consider the possiblity that the Federals could be trying to dig a mine under Confederate positions. This resulted in their failure to make any real effort to see what the Union was trying to do. Francis Lawley, the military correspondent of the London *Times*, assured Confederate leaders there was nothing to worry about. The longest military tunnel he knew about, dug during a siege in India, had been 400 feet (122 meters) long. Ventilation problems had made it impossible to go farther.

Despite these assurances, at least one Confederate officer did think something might be going on. Brigadier General Edward Porter Alexander, commander of artillery for the Confederate 1st Corps, noticed near the end of June that Union sharpshooters were keeping up a heavy fire across from Elliott's Salient, but fire had decreased on either side. Alexander thought the sharpshooters were trying to prevent Confederates from studying Union lines too carefully at this one point. Alexander later wrote:

> It was noticed that the sharpshooters' fire . . . was slackening . . . all along the line except at the Elliott Salient. Here the popping of muskets rather seemed to increase. . . . This satisfied me that something was going on there and that the next attempt of the Union would be made at that point.

On June 30, as he made more observations, Alexander realized what the Union were actually doing: "They were coming, but it was not above ground or it would show. They were mining us!"

As Alexander headed to Lee's headquarters to tell the general what he had found out, a Union sharpshooter shot Alexander. He would recover from the wound, but he went home to Georgia to recuperate. Before he left, Alexander spoke with one of Lee's aides about the possibility of a mine because Lee was not at headquarters. It was at this point that Francis Lawley said digging a tunnel that long was not possible. Even so, Lee ordered countermining—digging to try to hit, or at least hear, the Union diggers. Confederate efforts did not even start until July 15. They heard nothing. They did take measures to strengthen their lines near Elliott's Salient, though. Artillery pieces were put in place to cover the rear of the salient. A second trench was dug on a hill behind the salient.

On July 25, as a diversion from the mine and as an offensive movement in itself, Grant ordered Meade to prepare an offensive strike north of the James River. Winfield Scott Hancock, back in command of the II Corps, was to take his men and two divisions of cavalry and cross at Deep Bottom, ten miles (16 kilometers) southeast of Richmond. General Philip Sheridan would attack the city if this seemed viable. Otherwise, Sheridan was to take his cavalry and ride north and west around Richmond, destroying railroads. Hancock would advance on Chaffin's Bluff to prevent Confederate reinforcements from crossing the James and going after Sheridan. Hancock was also supposed to take advantage of any opportunity to advance directly on Richmond.

The move began late in the afternoon of June 26. The next morning Hancock turned west and ran into a strong enemy line at Bailey's Creek. When notified, Grant specifically forbade Hancock from attacking fortified positions. Hancock was told to hold his position for another day to support Sheridan's turning movement.

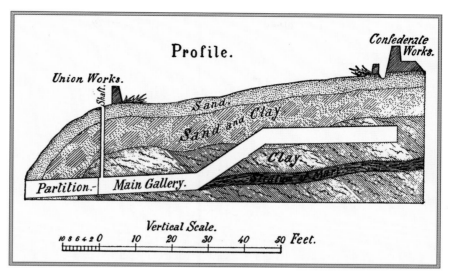

This diagram shows a cutaway side view of the Union shaft dug under Confederate positions.

This movement ended when Sheridan ran into a strong force of Confederate infantry. Grant reported the failure to Washington, D.C., but also realized that he had drawn away four of the seven Confederate divisions in the immediate area of Petersburg.

Grant had already ordered Meade to attack Petersburg directly, but nothing much was happening. Then, on June 26, Burnside submitted a plan of attack to follow the explosion of the mine. Two brigades would charge in columns through the gap left by the explosion. A regiment at the head of each column would peel off, to clear out the Confederates on either side of the fort. The rest of the lead division would head to Cemetery Hill, in back of the salient, followed by the rest of Burnside's corps. The plan had potential, but it would require the lead brigades to be prepared. The Confederates would recover from the shock of the blast, so the attack had to follow the explosion quickly.

On July 27, with the digging complete, Pleasants was told to start loading gunpowder into his mine. Four tons (four metric tons) of powder were loaded by hand into the cross shifts. This was less gunpowder than Pleasants had originally wanted to use, but it was all he could get from Meade's headquarters. In any event, the force of the blast would be better focused when the mineshaft was sealed. Pleasants also had another problem. Instead of one 98-foot (30-meter) continuous fuse, he had to make due with 10-foot (3-meter) lengths of fuse that he would have to splice together. It was all he could get from headquarters.

On Friday, July 29, Meade ordered Burnside's plan to begin the next day at 3:30 A.M. The V Corps would support Burnside's left and the II Corps his right. The relationship between Meade and Burnside had always been prickly. Meade had been Burnside's subordinate at Fredericksburg, when Burnside commanded the Army of the Potomac. So far, nothing very serious had happened to jeopardize the attack plan. Then, a major problem occurred. As historian Bruce Catton explained, "The Army of the Potomac was led to disaster many times, and there is a rather horrible fascination about tracing the steps by which, in each case, it reached that destination. Usually the steps seemed quite reasonable at the time."

Meade ordered Burnside to change his lead division. Burnside had wanted to use the division under General Edward Ferrero to lead the attack. This was Burnside's freshest division. The men had been stationed behind the lines and had been able to practice for the attack. They had never been in combat, though, and Meade wanted an experienced unit in the lead. Meade later told a court of inquiry that, "I understood that they had never been under fire; not that they should not be taken for such a critical operation as this, but that he [Burnside] should take such troops as from previous service could be depended upon as being perfectly reliable." Another issue was that the men in Ferrero's division were black, the only such unit in the Army of the Potomac. Meade was concerned that, if the division led the attack, it might look as if the commanders were trying to get the black troops killed.

When Burnside protested, Meade said he would talk to Grant. On Friday morning, less than 24 hours before the attack, Meade informed Burnside that Grant agreed that the lead division had to change. Additionally, Meade said, the movement to clear the enemy trenches would not be made. The attacking force would head straight toward Cemetery Hill, the second and more dominant Confederate position.

Now the serious problems began. Burnside was good at planning battles, but not so good when it came to carrying out his plans. He was terrible when he had to go into battle without sufficient time to plan. In this case, he had less than 24 hours to reorganize his attack plan.

Major-General Ambrose E. Burnside, commander of the Ninth Corps, Army of the Potomac, at the time of the Battle of the Crater. Burnside had commanded the Army of the Potomac at the Battle of Fredericksburg, two years before.

The Battle of the Crater

Such opportunity for carrying fortifications I have never seen and do not expect to have.

—Ulysses S. Grant to Henry Halleck, August 1, 1864

Burnside made another major error when he chose which of his three experienced divisions would lead the attack. He had the three brigadier generals commanding the divisions draw lots. Two of the generals were competent— Orlando Wilcox and Robert Potter. In fact, it was Potter who had forwarded the mining idea to Burnside in the first place. It was the third general who won the draw, however. This was James Ledlie, who may have been the worst general in the Army of the

Potomac. Ledlie was a heavy drinker and a poor commander. Ledlie was also considered, with justification, a
coward. As recently as the June 18 assaults on Petersburg,
when the Union still had a chance to take the city easily
and perhaps end the war, Ledlie had preferred to stretch
out on a safe patch of ground and drink while his men
charged the Confederate positions. Possibly not fully
realizing what a bad choice it was to have Ledlie lead the
attack, Burnside let the luck of the draw stand.

Burnside's second major mistake was to neglect to
prepare the path for his assault troops. Army headquarters
did not send the engineers it had promised, but Burnside
did not order his own engineers to find a way for his
men to get through or over his entrenchments, either. The
engineers would not go along during the assault to help
punch holes in the enemy works behind the expected hole
in the front lines. Burnside did not even give his troops
shovels and picks. All he did was order Ledlie to move first,
then Potter, and then Wilcox.

During the afternoon of July 29, with the explosion
set to take place early the next morning, Meade visited
Burnside's headquarters to stress the major weakness in
the plan. The shock of the explosion would buy the
Union only a brief opportunity for the attack. Meade
later said that he emphasized to the IX Corps commander and his subordinates that,

> This operation which we had to perform was one purely
> of time; that if immediate advantage was not taken of
> the explosion of the mine, and the consequent confusion
> of the enemy, and the crest immediately gained, it would
> be impossible to remain there; for, that as soon as the
> enemy should recover from their confusion, they would
> bring their troops and batteries to bear upon us and we
> would be driven out . . .

The men were ordered to attack quickly. If the attack did not work, they were to withdraw back to their own lines.

Colonel Pleasants entered the tunnel at 3:15 A.M. on Saturday, July 30, 1864, and lit the fuse. He then moved as rapidly as he could in the cramped quarters to get out of the tunnel before the gunpowder blew up. Fifteen minutes later, after the fuse should have burned the 98 feet (30 meters), nothing had happened. After 15 more minutes, the explosion had still not occurred. Anxious messages were coming in to Burnside's headquarters from Meade's headquarters. Pleasants was getting extremely nervous. He had to decide whether something had gone wrong or whether the fuse was just burning more slowly than expected. By 4:15 P.M., Pleasants finally allowed two very brave volunteers to go into the tunnel to see what had gone wrong.

They found that the fuse had gone out. They relit it and left as quickly as possible. The mine exploded at 4:40 A.M. William Powell, an officer on General Ledlie's staff, described what happened next:

> It was a magnificent spectacle, and as the mass of earth went up into the air, carrying with it men, guns, carriages, and timbers, and spread out like an immense cloud as it reached its altitude, so close were the Union lines that the mass appeared as if it would descend immediately upon the troops waiting to make the charge.

Another Union soldier later remembered, "a monstrous tongue of flame shot fully two hundred feet in the air, followed by a vast column of white smoke . . . then a great spout or fountain of red earth rose to a great height, mingled with men and guns, timbers and planks, and every kind of debris, all ascending, spreading, whirling, scattering and falling with great concussion to the earth once more." Confederate observers recorded similar impressions.

The way into Petersburg—and perhaps victory—was open, but it would not remain so for long. Powell wrote that it took ten minutes to reform the men, but that the cloud of debris would have prevented an attack sooner than that anyway. Then, the men had to get out of the trenches, primarily by forming steps up the trench walls with muskets. The soldiers had to advance to the crater a few men at the time, losing all order.

They raced 100 yards (91 meters) to the crater, climbed the 12-foot (4-meter) embankment formed by the explosion. The men then gaped at what lay before them. The Confederate position in the area had vanished. What was there now was a large hole, 200 feet (61 meters) long, 50 feet (15 meters) wide, and nearly 30 feet (9 meters) deep in the center. It was filed with guns, smashed carriages, timbers, and buried men, most of them—almost 300—dead, but a few trying to get free. After losing time just staring at the destruction, with follow-up units crowding from the rear, the leading regiment headed into the crater, rather than around it. Most of them helped wounded Confederates—an admirable action under other circumstances, but mistimed at this point—and many looked for souvenirs.

Part of the Union brigade commanded by Colonel Elisha Marshall, the second brigade of Ledlie's division, climbed out of the crater and lined up for a further advance. A heavy artillery regiment serving as infantry at that time found a working Confederate gun, turned it around, and began to fire at Confederate positions. The Union troops were using 160 guns to fire at Confederate positions near the crater, helping to suppress Confederate return fire and delay any counterattack.

When Marshall's men climbed out of the crater, they saw

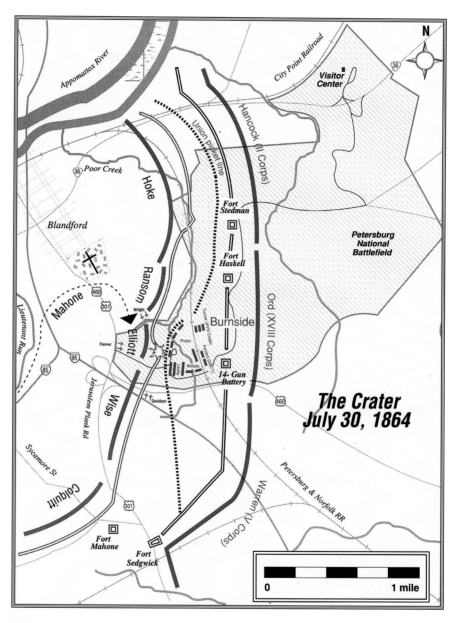

The Crater
July 30, 1864

Union troops dug a 500-foot shaft under Confederate positions, filled
the shaft with gunpowder, and blew a large hole in their positions.
Had the Union troops properly followed up, they would have had a good
chance of capturing Petersburg. This assault was subsequently called the
Battle of the Crater.

the very complex Confederate system of "communications" trenches. These covered pathways connected their rear positions with the front line. Many of them were at least partly filled with debris from the explosion. A few hundred yards beyond what one Union soldier called a "perfect honeycomb," the Union forces saw the newly built Confederate backup position, which provided a kind of back wall to the destroyed trench.

The Union troops did not have much time to contemplate the scene. The Confederates were beginning to respond, just as the Union high command had known they would. As early as 5:40 A.M., one hour after the explosion, messages discussing why the follow-up attack had not started began to pass from Meade to Burnside. Another series of telegrams included a message in which Burnside said he was doing all he could to get his men to advance. In reply, Meade asked if Burnside meant that his men would not obey his orders.

All the Union commanders were doing was cramming more and more men into a limited area near the crater. The Confederates soon had an excellent target—a general area so tightly packed that they could almost not help but hit somebody when they fired.

Confederate batteries were firing at the open ground between Union lines and the crater. One Confederate regiment was formed in a ditch running at right angles to the lines. They could hit the vulnerable flank of any Union forces forming in the open ground beyond the crater.

Robert E. Lee reached the area around 6:00 A.M. He sent word to William Mahone, who was in a quiet spot on the Confederate right, to send two brigades to reinforce the Confederates near the crater. Mahone, a commander whose aggressive style of fighting had been seen earlier at the Jerusalem Plank Road, decided to lead the brigades himself. When he arrived at the headquarters of Bushrod

Johnson, commander of the division holding the crater area, Johnson was at breakfast. Johnson had a junior officer lead Mahone and his men to the crater, and continued eating.

At least two of the four Union division commanders were more dramatically derelict in their duty than Johnson. James Ledlie was hiding in a bombproof at the back of the lines. A division commander's job was to coordinate his brigades, not to be in the front lines. Still, the division commander had to be close enough to see what was going on, in order to straighten out any problems, such as the massive confusion at the crater. Ledlie was not there, however. The divisions under Orlando Wilcox and Robert Potter just crowded in after Ledlie's men.

Ferrero had joined Ledlie, while his men piled into the confusion near the crater. The two generals asked a surgeon for a stimulant and issued an occasional order, but were not on hand when their men needed active leadership from commanders who would be able to adapt to confusion and changed circumstances. The men got nothing, not even any apparent concern for their safety.

Ledlie's aide Major William Powell later wrote that

> With the notable exception of General Robert B. Potter, there was not a division commander in the crater or connecting lines, nor was there a corps commander in the immediate scene of the action; the result being that the subordinate commanders attempted to carry out the orders issued prior to the commencement of the action, when the first attack developed the fact that a change of these plans was absolutely necessary.

Support for the attack from the V Corps on the left and the XIX Corps on the right was not coming. The V Corps remained inert. One division of the XIX Corps eventually did move forward, only to get swept back by a Confederate counterattack. The lack of leadership from most Union generals allowed the Union to waste nearly four hours during which only a few hundred men stood between the Union forces and Petersburg. Even a commander as good as Robert E. Lee would have been hard-pressed to save his army if Grant had split it in two.

Lee did not have to worry. As Johnson finished eating his breakfast and Ledlie and Ferrero kept drinking, Mahone was moving his two brigades toward the Union salient. At virtually the same moment that the brigades arrived on the scene, Colonel Henry G. Thomas, commanding one of Ferrero's brigades, managed to get 200 men out of the trench. They staged a bayonet charge against the advancing Confederates. Mahone then ordered one of his brigades to charge the oncoming Union troops.

When the charges met, the Confederates realized that they were fighting black troops. The battle then became particularly savage. Black troops were given no quarter—those who tried to surrender were usually shot or bayoneted. The Union finally broke and streamed back toward the crater. This flight touched off a similar retreat by part of the unit from the XIX Corps that had moved to support the main effort. The attack by the second of Mahone's brigades was not as successful as the first, but it eventually convinced the Union commanders that no further efforts were possible.

Meade ordered a total withdrawal at about 10:00 A.M. Little happened immediately. The units caught in the crater itself were left to fend for themselves. At that point, retreating was more dangerous than staying where they were. Confederate fire covered the open ground between the crater and the main Union lines quite effectively.

At 1:00 P.M., Mahone ordered his third brigade, which had just arrived, to charge the crater. A regiment from

A dead Confederate soldier in the trenches at the Confederate's Fort Mahone, called "Fort Damnation" by the soldiers on both sides. Fort Sedgwick, nearby on the Union side, was called "Fort Hell." This photograph was taken April 3, 1865, the day after Lee evacuated his lines at Petersburg and Richmond.

another division and a regiment from Elliott's brigade joined the charge. The Union troops were routed in a terrible slaughter. By 2:00 P.M., the Confederates had retaken the crater.

Grant reported the failure to Washington the next day:

The loss in the disaster of Saturday [is] about 3,500, of whom 450 men were killed and 2,000 wounded. It was the saddest affair I have witnessed in the war. Such opportunity for carrying fortifications I have never seen and do not expect to have. The enemy with a line of works five miles long had been reduced by our

African-American troops, from the 107th Regiment, United States Colored Troops, are shown posing outside a guardhouse at Fort Corcoran.

previous movements to the north side of James River to a force of only three divisions. This line was undermined and blown up, carrying a battery and most of a regiment with it. The enemy were taken completely by surprise and did not recover from it for more than an hour. . . . I am constrained to believe that had instructions been promptly obeyed that Petersburg would have been carried . . . without a loss of 300 men.

Burnside had not always obeyed instructions, as was pointed out later by the court of inquiry. He had also failed to take simple measures that would have made success more likely, such as sending engineers with the attacking troops. Burnside was not solely responsible for the failure, however. Others in the high command also contributed. Grant and Meade had not given the mine enough support. Gouvernor K. Warren, commanding the 5th Corps, and Edward O. C. Ord, commanding the XIX Corps, remained almost completely immobile, and did not supply the support and diversion that may have been vital. Three of the four division commanders, who should have been at the scene giving instructions, were not even there.

Clearly, the Army of the Potomac had not yet learned the need for proper coordination of its efforts, and had not been able to concentrate its potentially overwhelming resources. The Union army still did not seem to recognize the need for speed when dealing with Robert E. Lee. It would be nine months before an opportunity as good as that at the crater would occur.

Ambrose Burnside was relieved of command of the XIX Corps. He was replaced by John C. Parke, his chief of staff, rather than by Orlando Wilcox, the senior division commander who had been absent at the crater. James Ledlie, harshly censored by the court of inquiry, was sent on sick leave. He was never recalled to duty. Edward Ferrero, also severely censored for his conduct at the crater, managed to keep his job, and was transferred to command the defenses of the Bermuda Hundred. On the Confederate side, Billy Mahone was soon promoted to major general. He would stay with Lee until the end of the war as one of the South's best fighting generals.

Another Large Explosion and Some Offensive Moves

Union ships unload supplies at City Point in the autumn of 1864. City Point, formerly a small village in the James River, was the major Union supply center during the siege of Petersburg.

Had our troops behaved as they used to I could have beaten Hill.

—Winfield Scott Hancock to Orlando Wilcox, August 1864

The Petersburg front did not stay quiet for long after the disastrous Union attack at the crater. One particularly loud incident occurred just over a week later at City Point, Virginia, ten miles (16 kilometers) northeast of Petersburg.

The small village of City Point was located at the place where the Appomattox River met the James River. In 1838, a rail line was built to connect Petersburg and City Point. Although Petersburg was on the Appomattox River, the James was far more navigable. City Point, with regular steamboat service to New York City, became a port of entry for goods being shipped to Petersburg. Most of this commerce ended at the start of the Civil War due to the implementation of an increasingly effective Union blockade—particularly of the James River. What was left of City Point's commerce ended on May 5, 1864.

On May 5, the same day the Army of the Potomac entered the Wilderness, Union General Benjamin Butler's Army of the James landed at Bermuda Hundred. Some black troops were sent to occupy City Point. On June 15, General Grant arrived and made City Point his headquarters. The small village became the 1864 equivalent of the Pentagon.

By August 1864, City Point was not just Grant's headquarters. It was also the central distribution point for supplies to be used in the campaign against Petersburg and Richmond. It was more efficient to send supplies by ship than by land. The sea was also safer, since the Union had almost total control of the coastal waters. Land routes, on the other hand, posed the risk of danger from Confederate guerrillas. City Point had become a very busy port and supply center for two armies—and those armies needed huge amounts of supplies. For example, each day army animals alone required 600 tons (610 metric tons) of grain and oats.

City Point could not have been mistaken for a civilian port. Two lines of defensive positions protected the docks and supplies from an attack by land. Several ironclad gunboats were anchored in the James River north of the port with their guns pointing upriver, toward Richmond.

The army quartermaster and other supply departments remembered something about sieges. The attacker, as well as the defender, usually has supply problems. Union storage facilities at City Point kept 20 days' forage for the animals and a 30-day supply of rations for the soldiers on hand at all times. The Union troops also constructed a railroad, starting at the City Point docks and running behind the trenches to carry supplies directly to the armies at the front.

City Point was the center of a major war effort, but it was something else, too. City Point was a very tempting target. On July 26, 1864, before the explosion of the mine and the Battle of the Crater, John Maxwell, a Confederate secret agent, set out from Richmond. Another agent went with Maxwell; a man named R. R. Dillard. Maxwell carried what he called a "horological torpedo." This was a time bomb he had invented. He had orders to use it against Union vessels on the James. The agents' round-about route brought them to Norfolk, about 50 miles (81 kilometers) southeast of City Point. At Norfolk, they learned about the massive amounts of Union supplies held at City Point. They decided to go there and blow up one of the Union supply vessels.

August 9 was a Tuesday. The day was going to be exceedingly hot, even for a summer that had already been very hot and dry. One Union soldier recorded the temperature at 98°F (37°C), and this was at 6:30 A.M. Perhaps the distracting heat helped Maxwell and Dillard as they slipped through Union lines. They passed undetected through the Union picket line at City Point. Dillard hid at the outskirts of the port, while Maxwell went on with his torpedo. The bomb was actually a large box, probably not particularly noticeable, that contained somewhere between 12 and 15 pounds (5 to 7 kilograms) of explosives.

After arriving in the dock area, Maxwell saw the captain of one supply barge leave his vessel on an errand. Maxwell headed toward the barge. A sentry stopped him, so Maxwell said that the captain had ordered him to put the box on board. Maxwell then activated the bomb and gave it to a man from the barge to put on board. Maxwell and Dillard found a place to hide, in view of the barge but far enough away to be safe from the coming explosion. Maxwell had chosen his target well. The supply barge, the *J. E. Kendrick*, was loaded with ammunition.

A doctor named James Otis Moore was visiting City Point that day to pick up medical supplies. After completing his errand, Moore boarded the next train headed back to the front along with a companion. After some debate over whether they should sit inside in the heat or get some relief by riding on top of the car, they decided to stay inside. Other passengers chose to sit on the roof.

Morris Schaff, a Union staff officer, was in his office near the wharf when an old friend came to visit. They decided to walk the 100 yards (91 meters) to Grant's head-quarters to see an officer who had a well-stocked liquor cabinet. They found and joined in a card game. A female passenger, on a ship in the area, waiting for departure to Fort Monroe, decided it was too hot to stay inside. She headed up toward the open deck.

General Grant had just returned to City Point from a trip north. He was working outside in the morning heat, when he heard a report about an alleged Confederate infiltration of the city.

About 20 minutes before noon, the time bomb exploded. The *J. E. Kendrick* was totally obliterated. Another nearby barge blew up, as did a building on the wharf. A newsman at City Point felt the blast, and reported a sound like that of a cannon going off close to his ear. A soldier in the trenches, ten miles (16 kilometers) away, thought it sounded like a thunderclap. Another soldier saw a huge column of smoke.

Dr. Moore and his friend were looking in the direction of the explosion. Their eyes were filled with cinders from the blast before they could protect themselves. Moore and his companion emerged from the car into a horrible landscape of wreckage, bodies, and body parts. They immediately began to give medical aid where they could. The next day, Moore wrote to his wife that his decision to stay inside the car had probably saved his life.

A news reporter on the top of a railroad car was buffeted by the explosion, but curiously, was not knocked off the car. Another observer noticed how weapons, bullets, wood, and other scrap shot through the air with tremendous, and potentially deadly, force. This observer, who had taken shelter under his wagon, had to devote most of his attention to avoiding the hoofs of his panicked horse.

The woman ship passenger, seeking comfort on deck, arrived just a few seconds after the explosion to see bodies and equipment flying through the air. Then, a man's severed head fell at her feet. She picked it up by the hair and placed it in a nearby bucket of water. The woman later reported that a large bakery had been completely destroyed. All that remained was a chimney, with an anchor and chain perched on top.

Schaff's card game came to an abrupt halt. A cannonball ripped into the tent, and smashed a trunk that lay in the center of the circle of officers. The men all left quickly, although Schaff did return to take a look at what had happened. Schaff saw "a staggering scene, a mass of overthrown buildings, their timbers tangled into almost impenetrable heaps."

Grant's aide Horace Porter recalled an explosion with a sound "Which vividly recalled the Petersburg mine. . . . Then there rained down upon the party a terrific shower of shells, bullets, boards and fragments of timber. The general was surrounded by splinters and various kinds of ammunition, but fortunately was not touched by any of the missiles."

Aides remarked that Grant's composure did not change at all. He seemed to be the only one unaffected

Lieutenant-General Ulysses S. Grant, June 1864, at Cold Harbor. Grant usually wore a private's uniform jacket (a single row of buttons) with his general's stars on each shoulder. Interestingly, no photograph of him in his actual field uniform seems to exist.

by the explosion. Later estimates were that $2 million (in the money of the time) worth of supplies and property had been destroyed. At least 43 people were killed and 126 people were wounded, although the number of dead was probably higher. There was no way of counting the number of unregistered black laborers who were vaporized by the force of the blast.

Soon after the explosion, a court of inquiry ruled that the incident was an accident. Even so, security was tightened. The ammunition depot was rebuilt far away from the main wharf. Maxwell's role in the incident remained a mystery for years. After the war, John Maxwell went to see Grant's aide Orville Babcock. By then, Grant had been elected president of the United States. Babcock had been on Grant's staff during the Civil War, including at City Point, and had come with him to the White House. Maxwell complained to Babcock about the treatment he was getting from the patent office. Trying to convince Babcock of his skill as an inventor, Maxwell told him about the horological torpedo he had invented, and how it had worked that day at City Point. Babcock described the incident, writing that "I told him that his efforts, from his standpoint, had been eminently successful."

Conventional military operations picked up again four days after the City Point explosion. In early August, Grant learned that Lee had sent reinforcements to the Shenandoah Valley to fight the Union troops under Philip Sheridan. This information was only partly correct. Lee had in fact sent an infantry division, a cavalry division, and artillery to the valley. However, Richard Anderson, Confederate 1st Corps commander, was in charge of the units. Not as many Confederates had left Petersburg as Grant thought.

Grant decided to take advantage of this apparent

opportunity. Winfield Scott Hancock would take his II Corps and part of the Army of the James—the X Corps, under David Bell Birney—and move on Richmond from the Union right. Grant began his offensive with an attempt at deception. Hancock's men were loaded onto ships at City Point on August 13, 1864, and sailed down the James, away from Richmond, to try to distract Confederate attention from the intended target.

Cornelia Hancock, a Quaker nurse with the II Corps (no relation to General Hancock), wrote to her mother a few days later: "On the 11th orders were received for the Corps to come to City Point and be shipped in transports without any destination assigned them. They were all jubilant thinking they were going to Washington." They were not.

Hancock's men were actually headed south down the James River, where they would sit and wait until dark. The troops would then reverse course and head past City Point to a place called Curles Neck, five miles (eight kilometers) from Richmond, at a bend in the river known as Deep Bottom, because it was the deepest part of the James. The men would land across from a bridgehead the Union controlled north of the James. A thrust at Richmond would follow after they crossed the river. The Union troops assumed they would be attacking weakened Confederate positions. They thought they could take the city, split Lee's lines, and possibly end the war. At the very least, Lee would have to call back some of the troops he had sent to the Shenandoah Valley.

The process of loading the transports and getting them to the rendezvous point took from noon into the evening. Darkness provided security, but it also made for a long wait on hot ships. An aide to General Hancock wrote, "Suffocatingly hot to night on board the crowded steamers. Almost impossible to get any sleep. The mosquitoes infernally tormenting."

The weather and loading time were not the only factors that would make the men tired, if not exhausted, by the time they landed. Union staff workers were once again engaged in their unfortunate habit of messing up good ideas. Grant's staff, which handled the planning, was used to the rivers of the western United States. The rivers of the West are very powerful, capable of changing course by digging new paths for themselves. They are not subject to tidal action, which can quickly erode banks. A river landing, particularly uncontested, could be done with gangplanks from steamers alone. That was not so on the James. Getting off the steamers would require the men to transfer to smaller boats or use wharves.

Hancock's maneuver force did not have smaller vessels. The two wharves they found at Deep Bottom were wrecked (no one had checked) and had to be rebuilt. They were rebuilt relatively quickly, but still, this delayed the troops from disembarking until mid-morning. In the meantime, the Confederates were able to prepare to respond to the threat. To make matters worse, the men would have to march during the hottest part of the day, which would cause a major problem if men fell victim to heat exhaustion. The Union would also have to advance around a creek, which would also slow the troops down.

Birney's X Corps would cross one of two Union bridges closer to Richmond and attack Confederate positions near Deep Bottom. The II Corps and an accompanying cavalry division, would cross on the eastern Union bridge. A division of that corps would attack to the west of a creek that split the battle area. The other two units would attack to the east. The cavalry division would protect the Union right. If all went well, the cavalry would try to get around the Confederate left and wreck some railroads.

Postwar photograph of a pontoon bridge across the James River at Deep Bottom, Virginia. Union engineers were experts at quickly building temporary pontoon bridges.

The attacks on August 14 accomplished little. Birney scored some gains, but only against modest opposition. One of the three II Corps divisions attacked as ordered. A second division from the II Corps, under Francis Barlow, attacked piecemeal. Barlow failed to concentrate his forces against Confederate positions near Fussell's Mill and to move up the weakly defended Darbytown Road. Barlow, normally a tough and effective combat commander, was ill that day, suffering from the lingering effects of a serious wound he had received at Gettysburg. He was also worried about his ailing wife. Barlow's failure was not unique, though. Problems with coordinating and focusing attacks were chronic among the Union forces.

The next day, Hancock planned to move Birney's X Corps from the left to the right center, to attack at Fussell's Mill. Birney was supposed to have his men in position for a 6:00 A.M. attack. They did not all arrive until 1:00 P.M. Birney then spent the next six hours scouting and studying the Confederate left. He informed Hancock that he would make a vigorous attack the next morning.

Union cavalry started their attack on their right early the morning of August 16. They made good progress at first, even against near-constant skirmishing with Confederate forces. At one point, the Union troops shot and killed a Confederate cavalry commander. As they searched the body, they found a detailed map of the Richmond defenses.

Union cavalry forces flanked and penetrated to the rear of a Confederate division. By 1:30 P.M., however, increasingly heavy Confederate counterattacks first stopped and then drove back this advance. The situation only got worse when a supporting Union infantry brigade was withdrawn and sent to help the Union infantry attack in the center.

Birney had planned to launch the main Union attack at the same time as the cavalry attack. However, when dawn came, Birney decided that the point he had selected for his attack would not work. The Union forces spent the next four hours looking for a place to attack. They finally decided on a site northeast of the millpond at Fussell's Mill.

The attack did not start until late morning. General Charles Field, in command of Confederate forces in the area, heard sharp firing at 10:00 A.M. The firing only lasted a few minutes before it settled down to the kind of intermittent fire characteristic of skirmishing. A few hours later, the heavy firing started again.

The Union troops broke through Confederate lines about noon. Unfortunately for the Union troops, they did not clear Confederate lines on either side of the breakthrough. The Union column took fire on both sides. Fighting at the front was hand-to-hand. The Union column was eventually hit by strong Confederate counterattacks, as units were sent to reinforce Field. By mid-afternoon, Field was able to stage a coordinated counterattack, which drove the Union troops virtually back to their starting point.

The Union left flank, the II Corps under Hancock's direct control, played little part in that day's fighting. That night, August 17, Grant reported that fighting was favorable but that there had been no decisive results.

That same evening, Grant determined that, since Lee was sending reinforcements north of the James, it might be an appropriate time for an attack south of the James. The next day, General G. K. Warren was told to move his V Corps, stationed near the left of the Union lines, to the Weldon Railroad and to do as much damage as possible.

Warren's advance started on August 18. His troops were attacked on August 19 and forced back part of the way to their starting point. A second Confederate attack the next day failed to dislodge the V Corps. Warren had reestablished contact with the main Union lines. His raid resulted in a permanent extension of the Union lines. The Confederates could still use the Weldon Railroad, but now they had to travel 20 miles (32 kilometers) farther by wagon between their lines and the portion of the railroad they still controlled.

August 17 was when Grant received the message from

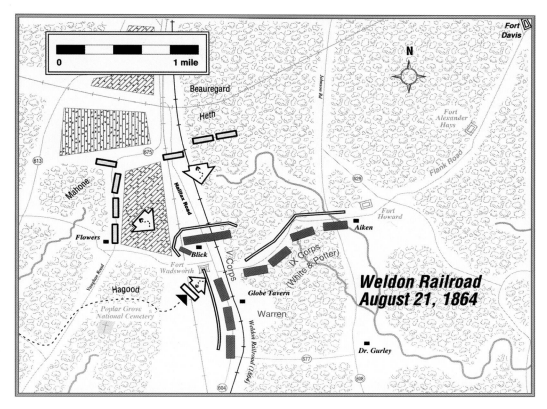

The Weldon Railroad operation, a Union strike on one of the two remaining working Confederate rail lines, was part of continuing Union efforts to cut Confederate supplies. The Union line extended to cut the railroad at this point. Lee was able to use the wagons to bring supplies from further down the Weldon railroad line, but it was that much harder for Lee's army to get what it needed to survive.

Lincoln advising him to hold on with a bulldog grip. Grant liked the message. He commented to his aides that Lincoln had more nerve than his advisors.

Progress was being made at Petersburg and other fronts. Lee was slowly being weakened. On August 18, the same day Warren made his advance, just how much Lee had begun to falter was seen when Lee tried to organize a major assault on Hancock's force. Lee's attacks started late and had little success. Hancock's troops, finally withdrawn two days later, did not face much real danger.

Still, Union advancement was not readily apparent. The three main Union offensives—Petersburg, the Shenandoah Valley, and Georgia—seemed stalemated. General William T. Sherman was winning battles, aided by the tendency of the new commanding general of the Confederate Army of Tennessee, John Bell Hood, to attack constantly. Hood still held Atlanta, Georgia, though. At the same time, Sheridan seemed to be maneuvering to avoid battle in the Shenandoah Valley. Lastly, in Petersburg, a continuing series of unsuccessful Union thrusts always seemed to be blunted by expert Confederate responses.

Lincoln needed nerve to take a bold step in the war. August 1864 was the lowest point of the Union war

Life in Petersburg During the Siege

During the siege of Petersburg, the Union armies were actually targeting the Confederate forces defending the town. Union efforts to cut supply lines to Lee's army in order to starve the Confederates out had an effect on civilians in Petersburg as well as members of the military.

Sarah Pryor, a Petersburg resident and the wife of former U.S. Congressman Roger Pryor, wrote of efforts to cope with food shortages and high inflation: "With all our starvation we never ate rats, mice or mule-meat. We managed to exist on peas, bread, and sorghum. We could buy a little milk, and we mixed it with a drink made from roasted and ground corn. The latter, in the grain, was scarce."

A visitor to the city wrote of the more drastic effects on the lives of refugees from the countryside with no friends or relatives in town: "I have since I have been around Petersburg, seen many poor women and children compelled to go among the soldiers and beg for bread to eat."

effort. It was also the time at which Lincoln was most unpopular. On August 23, 1864, Lincoln, expecting defeat in the November presidential election, had his cabinet members sign a folded piece of paper without letting them read it first. On the paper, which Lincoln put away in a drawer of his desk, he had written,

> This morning, as for some days past, it seemed exceedingly possible that this Administration will not be re-elected. Then it will be my duty to so-cooperate with the President elect, as to save the Union between the election and the inauguration; as he will have secured his election on such ground that he cannot possibly save it afterwards.

The Winter

Major General George Meade
is shown with senior staff and
subordinate field commanders in
1865. Left to right are Brigadier
General George Macy, Major
General Alexander S. Webb,
Major General Andrew A.
Humphreys, Major General
Charles Griffin, Meade, Major
General John G. Parke, and
Major General Henry J. Hunt.

*When I see and hear the misery occasioned all over the land, my
heart shudders and bleeds. What next? Heaven knows.*

—Wife of a Georgia officer in the Army of Northern
Virginia to her husband, February 1865

n August 22, Nelson Miles, in temporary command of
Barlow's division of the II Corps, was told to make
another drive at the Weldon Railroad. A regiment of
Union cavalry scouted down to Reams Station, on the same railroad,
but found no Confederates. The next day, another division from
the II Corps was sent to reinforce Barlow, now back in command
of his division.

That same day, Wade Hampton, in command of all of Lee's cavalry, personally scouted Union deployments near Ream's Station. He informed Lee that an attack was feasible. Lee was concerned about having his men attack so far from the Confederate trench system. Yet, he also realized that he needed to protect the railroad, and he knew that a Confederate victory would help discredit the Lincoln administration. Lee decided to go ahead with the attack. The 3rd Corps commander, A. P. Hill, would command eight brigades of infantry, plus Hampton's two cavalry divisions. This was as large a force as Lee could spare.

Hill's force headed out to the southwest. The force would swing around and try to attack Hancock from three directions: infantry from the west, and cavalry from the south and east. Union signalmen spotted the Confederate movement and notified Grant and Meade. Meade informed Hancock of a possible Confederate attack against the II Corps. Hancock, however, would not get reinforcements. He would have to make do with the forces he had. Hancock was also not given the option of withdrawing his command.

Hancock's men found Union positions built in late June, at the time of the Jerusalem Plank Road operation, an L-shaped position that faced north and west. Hancock decided to add positions to cover a possible attack on Ream's Station from the south. The result was a cramped position that formed almost a complete circle.

About 8:00 A.M. on August 25, Hampton's cavalry struck Union cavalry outposts south of the main Union position. Heavy fighting ensued, with elements of one of the II Corps divisions reinforcing the hard-pressed Union cavalry. About 2:00 P.M. the Union began to withdraw back toward Ream's Station. About this time, Confederate infantry began to approach from the west. The first Confederate attack had been repulsed.

The second Confederate attack began at about 4:00 P.M. A few minutes earlier, Hancock received a message from Meade that reinforcements were on the way—but by a somewhat roundabout route. Hancock replied to Meade that he thought he could hold Ream's Station until nightfall. Hancock heard from another courier, just after the second Confederate attack was fought off, that Meade was sending another division, but also by an indirect route.

The third Confederate attack began at about 5:15 P.M. It was preceded by a 15-minute artillery bombardment. The Union seemed to be defeating this attack, as well. Then, suddenly, and inexplicably, three regiments at the northern part of the Union line broke ranks and fled. Confederate troops took advantage of the weakness and quickly began to climb over the Union breastworks. In the past, the rout of one part of a Union line could destroy the whole position. That no longer happened, but still the integrity of the line was gone. The Union held on to what remained of their position until 9:00 P.M., when Hancock reluctantly gave the order to withdraw.

The Confederates were in no position to retreat. They concentrated on recovering captured weapons and rounding up prisoners. Over three-quarters of the 2,600 Union casualties were missing or captured, an appalling number for a unit with the history and reputation of the II Corps.

Reams Station was another failed Union move at Petersburg. It did cost Lee more casualties that he could not easily afford, though Lee lost only about a quarter of Hancock's total casualties. Elsewhere, however, Union efforts began to show concrete results. About a week after Reams Station, William Sherman took Atlanta. Then, Philip Sheridan defeated Jubal Early at Winchester in the Shenandoah Valley on September 19, and at Fisher's Hill three days later.

Heavy campaigning at Petersburg came to the end in the late fall. However, some significant developments occurred in the next few months. Winfield Scott Hancock left the Army of the Potomac in November 1864. Lincoln was reelected president on November 8, 1864, with heavy support from soldiers in the field. Benjamin Butler was relieved of command in January. A Union victory was now just a matter of time. Still, there was a long winter to get through.

Both sides tried to improve their camps, doing what they could to convert temporary into at least semipermanent and semicomfortable quarters. The Union troops were more successful. They were well supplied and well fed, thanks in large part to the railroad from City Point. The Union troops could sense victory. They believed the spring campaign would finally bring an end to the war. Near the end of the winter, in fact, an interesting trend developed. Union veterans who had been discharged in 1864, after their three-year terms were up, began to rejoin the army. They wanted to be part of the Union forces at the successful close of the war.

Lee's supply situation was getting worse. Interestingly, the Confederacy as a whole actually had most of the supplies its armies needed. It was difficult, however, to get those supplies to their armies, particularly the Army of Northern Virginia, which was in constant close contact with the Union. Grant's raids on Southern supply routes to Petersburg and Richmond were having the effect he desired.

The rate of desertion from Lee's army increased. Men did not want to die for a cause that seemed to be lost. News from home, particularly from families who lived in the path of Sherman's destructive "March to the Sea" from Atlanta to Savannah, Georgia, made the soldiers' morale even worse. Although the reports made many soldiers angry, determined never to give in to the Northerners who had wreaked havoc on their home state, for most, the knowledge of what their families must be going through steadily sapped their will to fight. Even the most dedicated

This photograph shows the interior of Fort Stedman. The last Confederate attack, March 25, 1865, occurred at this fort. The Confederates briefly broke through but were not able to maintain their success. They were pushed back with heavy casualties.

soldier would have a hard time going on if it were his wife being described in the journal of Mary Gay, a Georgia refugee, *Life in Dixie During the War*. She wrote of having seen in Decatur, Georgia, "a young mother, beautiful in desolation, with a baby in her arms, and on either side of her, a little one, piteously crying for something to eat. . . . She could only give them soothing words." (Fortunately, Mary Gay was able to find food to give to the woman and her children.)

There was still hope for a successful end to the war, no matter how unrealistic, among the people of Richmond. A woman living there during the Civil War later wrote, "To those who reflected upon our situation in all its bearings, though it was evidently desperate and discouraging, there seemed no necessity for subjugation. We earnestly looked forward to the spring campaign. We relied on the grand old Army of Northern Virginia to retrieve the reverses of the last few months. . . ." However, she continued, "Richmond was now almost destitute of provisions."

One battle of note took place during the winter. Grant was receiving intelligence reports that wagon traffic on the Boydton Plank Road, running from Petersburg south to the area suppling Lee's army, was heavy. He decided to take advantage of good weather to capture Confederate wagon trains and limit or even deny use of this route to Lee. A Union cavalry division was sent on a wide southwest sweep to Dinwiddie Court House to reach the road and to capture or destroy any Confederate traffic found along the way. The II Corps and the V Corps were ordered to support the cavalry move and to take advantage of any other opportunities that arose.

The Union cavalry division moved out on schedule on the morning of February 5, 1865. The troops found few wagons on the Boydton Plank Road, however. After completing what little it could do, the cavalry was ordered to fall back. Andrew A. Humphreys had replaced Hancock in command of the II Corps back in November. On February 5, he took two divisions of his corps and moved to within 1,000 yards (914 meters) of the closest Southern positions, near Hatcher's Run, a small creek that gave its name to the operation. The Union line faced north and the Confederate line faced south. A Southern attack that afternoon was driven off, but Humphreys was later reinforced.

The V Corps had taken a position to the south of the II Corps, but with its lines facing west and slightly south. Both corps formed a bulge in the Union lines. This concerned George Meade. He ordered both corps and the cavalry to concentrate near the II Corps position at Hatcher's Run. The next morning, February 6, all units were ordered to probe outward to try to determine the enemy's location. The II Corps found no Confederate forces until it got to the main enemy works. The V Corps was late getting started. Union cavalry ran into a Confederate division under John Pegram, and a sharp fight ensued.

The fighting grew more intense on the Union right flank when a second Confederate division appeared and entered the battle. Union reinforcements met this threat, but then the Confederate division under William Mahone appeared and staged the hard-hitting attack typical of men under Mahone's command. The Union troops were forced back. Their withdrawal stopped only when additional Union reinforcements arrived. The battle ended when night fell.

Casualties were relatively light. General John Pegram, who was in his early thirties, was killed on February 6. He had recently been married in Richmond. A few days after the battle, many of the same guests who had attended his wedding were back in the same church for his funeral.

The Battle of Hatcher's Run was indecisive. The Union showed that it still had not worked out its constant problems with timing and coordinating operations among different units. Union lines were successfully extended, however, and Lee's supply situation became a little worse.

The Confederate government made several last-ditch moves in these weeks. From January 29 to 31, a Confederate delegation met for peace talks with a group of Union representatives, including President Lincoln himself. The talks failed. Neither the Confederates nor Lincoln were willing to compromise their stance on independence or slavery. On January 31, 1865, Congress passed the Thirteenth Amendment to the Constitution, ending slavery in the United States.

On January 26, 1865, Confederate President Jefferson Davis signed an act of the Confederate Congress that created the post of general-in-chief. Five days later, the Confederate Senate quickly confirmed Davis's nomination of Robert E. Lee for the new post. Then, amazingly, on March 13, 1865, Davis signed into law an act that authorized the recruitment of blacks into the Confederate army.

While these political developments took place, on March 7, 1865, Lee sent James Longstreet detailed instructions about how to carry out his retreat from Richmond and Petersburg. One choice Lee still had to make was where to retreat once he withdrew from Petersburg and Richmond. He could head west. He could also head south to North Carolina, joining with Joseph Johnston's army in an attempt to stop William Sherman's northward advance. Johnston could do nothing alone, and if Lee delayed too long, Sherman would come to him.

Securing a route for retreat south or west from Petersburg was the primary reason for the attack on the Union Fort Stedman, a mile (1.5 kilometers) south of the Appomattox River, near the center of the Petersburg lines, planned for March 29, 1865. Some Confederates officials, particularly Secretary of War John C. Breckinridge, also hoped that keeping Lee's army in the field as long as possible might allow the Confederacy to get better terms from the Union than the unconditional surrender it currently demanded. Lee, always an aggressive commander, felt the need to make one last effort.

John Gordon, commanding Lee's 2nd Corps, would have about half the army to use in the attack. If the assault worked, the Union left, curving south of Petersburg, might have to withdraw. Lee and his army would have a relatively clear path to retreat west and southwest from Petersburg.

The plan was a good one. The first step was to gain some local surprise on the Union forces by taking advantage of a continuing Union effort to encourage Confederates to desert and bring their rifles with them. The Union paid ten dollars to each Confederate who arrived with a rifle, depriving the South of equipment as well as manpower.

About 4:00 A.M. on March 25, 1865, Union pickets in front of Fort Stedman saw some Confederates approaching out of the darkness. Their rifles were reversed, with the barrel down and stock up, according to the usual procedure. The Union pickets thought the men were more Southern deserters—until the Southerners turned their rifles back to normal combat stance and took the Union soldiers prisoner.

Several handpicked Confederate companies of 100 men each quickly took Fort Stedman. One staff officer from the Union IX Corps, the unit that held the lines near Fort Stedman, was sent to investigate what was going on at the fort. He tried to give orders to the men he saw at the fort, until the light of the dawn showed him the color of the uniforms they were wearing.

The first follow-up Confederate units had some success as they spread out to the right and the left. Some Union trenches were captured. More Confederates came in to try to hold the captured positions.

Then, the assault began to go wrong. Three 100-man companies had been assigned to take positions to cover Fort Stedman in the second line of Union defenses. Their guides got lost in the dark of the complex Union trench system. The first Union counterattack was fought off. Supporting troops had not arrived. By dawn, Gordon and Lee already knew they had to withdraw. A second Union attack helped send the Confederates back to their starting point, with fairly heavy casualties.

Union attacks on the left by the II and VI Corps managed to capture some of the Confederate pickets but were unable to make a dent in the main Confederate positions. The Fort Stedman attack had made no major difference in the situation around Petersburg. The assault did not delay Grant's intended swing around the Confederate right.

End Game

Shown here is a group of Confederate prisoners captured at the Battle of Five Forks, April 1, 1865. Union victory at this battle forced Lee's evacuation of Petersburg. Confederate uniforms appear darker than expected. Most Confederate enlisted men wore what was known as "butternut" brown uniforms, rather than the official gray.

Lieutenant-General Grant: Gen. Sheridan says "If the thing is pressed, I think Lee will surrender," Let the thing be pressed.

—Abraham Lincoln to Ulysses S. Grant, April 7, 1865

ne crucial element of Grant's swing around the Confederate right, was the cavalry under Philip Sheridan, which had just returned after a campaign in the Shenandoah Valley. The second element was the V Corps and II Corps of the Army of the Potomac, along with three divisions from the Army of the James, pulled out of line and secretly moved down to the Union left. Grant had nine infantry divisions with 54,000 men and three cavalry divisions with 13,000 men, for a combined force in that wing that was larger than Lee's entire remaining army.

The Union troops move began on March 29. Sheridan and the cavalry took a wide swing around the end of Lee's lines and headed for Dinwiddie Court House. The V Corps took a more direct route to the White Oak Road. The II Corps and the troops from the Army of the James extended the left of the Union lines.

The first Confederate resistance came that same day at a place known as Lewis Farm, near the Quaker Road. The battle started at a place called Gravely Run. Part of Bushrod Johnson's Confederate division was defending a position just across the shallow creek. The commander of the lead brigade of the Union V Corps, Joshua Lawrence Chamberlain, quickly brushed aside Confederate opposition. The Southerners retreated back to their position at Lewis Road.

Then, Chamberlain attacked the Confederates at Lewis Road. He was driven back, but was able to divert the Confederates enough so that Warren and the rest of the V Corps were able to extend the Union lines. Johnson's division retreated at dusk to White Oak Road. Warren's men now held the Boydton Plank Road, one of Lee's last supply lines and Lee's only direct connection with a maneuver force under George Pickett.

Sheridan's cavalry reached Dinwiddie Court House late on March 29. There, Sheridan received instructions from Grant to head north to the Five Forks, a highly strategic road junction. If he held Five Forks, Sheridan would be in a position to cut the two remaining railroads into Petersburg. Lee would have no choice but to leave. Sheridan sent a cavalry division to try to take Five Forks that night. Confederates under George Pickett held the junction, so the Union division withdrew slightly

The next day, March 30, heavy rains made a Union advance all but impossible. On March 31, Sheridan and the cavalry would go after Five Forks once again. G. K. Warren's V Corps would head for White Oak Road to cut off the route Lee needed to reinforce Pickett.

The Confederates struck first. Infantry under Pickett and cavalry under Fitzhugh Lee attacked Sheridan from the west. Sheridan, who had only four brigades in the immediate area of combat, was forced back. Sheridan sent a message to Grant, saying that he would likely be forced back from Dinwiddie Court House. A second message, delivered in person to Horace Porter, was more positive. Porter quoted Sheridan as saying that he would be able to hold Dinwiddie. Sheridan then added, referring to Pickett, Fitz Lee, and their men, that "This force is in more danger than I am. If I am cut off from the Army of the Potomac, it is cut off from Lee's army, and not a man in it ought ever to be allowed to get back to Lee. We have at least drawn the enemy's infantry out of its fortifications, and this is our chance to attack it."

The Battle of White Oak Road, which took place at almost the same time, proved Sheridan's point. The V Corps under Warren had been advancing to Sheridan's right, but with no direct connection. In the late morning, Warren was attacked and forced back by a smaller Confederate force. He managed to recover in the afternoon, pushing the Southern force back to its main White Oak Road line. Warren saw that the line was too strong for an immediate attack. What mattered more, though, was that Warren was now between Lee and his last available maneuver force.

Grant and Sheridan could see that despite the apparent danger to Sheridan's force, they could destroy Pickett by using Warren's corps. Carrying out this move, however, caused a series of sometimes confusing and contradictory orders to be sent to Warren. Some orders arrived out of sequence. One particularly unfortunate message from Grant to Sheridan, assured Sheridan that the V Corps would arrive around midnight. This would have been a realistic estimate only if the V Corps had already been assembled and ready to move. The corps, however, was still in close contact with the enemy, and not at all ready to move.

The Union made contact with some of Pickett's men. Pickett now knew the Union troops were at his rear. He started to withdraw north to Hatcher's Run. However, Lee ordered Pickett to hold Five Forks. Pickett placed his men in an L-shaped position along the White Oak Road, with the longer part of the L facing south. Pickett's left, the short arm of the L, angled northward. The gap between Pickett's left and the nearest part of Lee's main line, under Anderson, was supposed to be covered by a small brigade under William P. Roberts, then the youngest general in the Confederate army.

Sheridan, never the most patient of men, was anxiously awaiting Warren's arrival. Warren's corps did not arrive until morning. When the troops finally got there, Warren was at the rear, personally supervising withdrawal from close contact with Confederate forces. He delayed reporting to Sheridan for about three hours.

After further delays in getting the V Corps getting into position, the Union attack did not start until 4:15 P.M. on April 1. The plan was to strike hard at the angle where Pickett's line turned north. The problem was that Pickett was not where Sheridan and Warren thought he was. As a result, the V Corps headed off into empty space. The left of the V Corps, the division under Romain Ayres started taking fire on its left flank. Ayres realized the problem, turned left, and attacked the Confederates. Samuel Crawford's division, on the right, kept going, opening a gap.

Charles Griffin, behind the other two divisions, moved to fill the gap. By 5:30 P.M., Ayres and Griffin had crushed Confederate defenses on the left. Warren was chasing

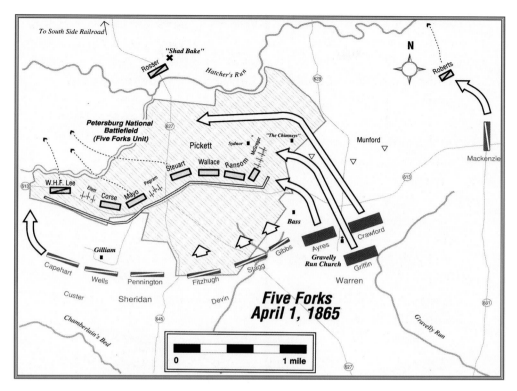

To South Side Railroad

"Shad Bake"

Rosser

Hatcher's Run

N

Roberts

628

Petersburg National
Battlefield
(Five Forks Unit)

627

Pickett

Sydnor

"The Chimneys"

McGregor

Munford

Mackenzie

Steuart

Wallace

Ransom

613

W.H.F. Lee

Ellett

Corse

Mayo

Pegram

613

Bass

Gilliam

Capehart

Wells

Pennington

Fitzhugh

Stagg

Gibbs

Ayres

Gravelly
Run Church

Crawford

Griffin

Custer

Sheridan

Devin

Warren

**Five Forks
April 1, 1865**

Chamberlain's Bed

645

Gravelly Run

651

627

0

1 mile

Grant sent Sheridan, with a combined cavalry and infantry force, on a broad sweep around the Confederate right flank. On the afternoon of April 1, 1865, the commanders of the Confederate right wing were enjoying a shad (fish) bake behind the lines. Sheridan attacked and destroyed a Confederate force holding the strategic Five Forks crossroads. The next day, Grant ordered attacks all along the Confederate lines. Union breakthroughs at several points forced Lee to order an immediate evacuation of Petersburg.

Crawford, whom he eventually found and turned around. Crawford's division hit Pickett's line in the rear, capturing a large number of prisoners and sending the rest retreating to the west, away from Lee's army.

Warren was dealing with Sheridan, who became angry when he could not find Warren. Using authority Grant had given him, Sheridan relieved Warren of his command and replaced him with Griffin. Sheridan was probably not being fair to Warren. However, as historian Bruce Catton later put it,

> This was the first time in the history of the Army of the Potomac that a ranking commander has been summarily fired because his men had been put into action tardily and inexpertly. Sheridan had been cruel and unjust—and if that cruel and unjust insistence on driving, aggressive promptness had been the rule in this army from the beginning, the war probably would have been won two years earlier.

On the Confederate side, Lee's commanders in the area, Pickett, Fitz Lee, and Richard Anderson, were attending a shad (a kind of fish) bake behind the lines. The battle was virtually over by the time they knew anything was wrong.

About 9:00 P.M., Grant learned of the great success. He now had Union forces behind Lee's army. He then ordered a general assault along all the Petersburg and Richmond lines. Breakthroughs occurred in several places, slicing up the Southern defenses. One break was made on the right of Lee's main lines when the Union VI Corps scored a notable success against A. P. Hills's Confederate 3rd Corps. Lee was at his headquarters conferring with Hill and 1st Corps commander James Longstreet when he learned of the Union success. Hill left to try to repair the situation with his own corps. He and an aide saw two Union soldiers and attempted to capture them. The Union soldiers took shelter behind a tree, aimed their rifles, and fired. One of them shot Hill through the heart. He was probably dead before he hit the ground.

Lee learned of Hill's death about the same time that he realized the situation at Petersburg could not be fixed. The siege was over. Petersburg and Richmond would fall to the Union. A few hours later, while he was sitting in church,

Jefferson Davis received a message from Lee. It informed the president that Richmond would have to be evacuated that night. Lee's first concern now was to save his army. After that, he would decide what to do with his troops.

Sheridan's victory at Five Forks had cut off that route for a Confederate retreat. Lee's forces at Petersburg, forced back to a line of inner defense works that had been created for such an emergency situation, would first have to retreat northward over the few bridges across the Appomattox River, and then head west. Union forces would have to be held off until nighttime. Despite heavy Union attacks, the Confederates did manage to hold their positions until nightfall.

The Army of Northern Virginia and the Confederate government left Richmond that evening. The government headed southwest, and the army went almost directly west. Lee's intention was first to get away from Grant's closely pressing army, and then to reach supplies, particularly food, that he had been told were waiting to the west at Amelia Court House. Lee then planned to swing south to try to hook up with Joseph Johnston's Confederate army in North Carolina.

Law and order left Richmond with the army and the government. The chaos increased when fires from strategic materials that Lee had ordered to have burned, and from burning government papers, spread out of control. Frightened residents began to loot stores and homes. A Confederate cavalry officer in charge of one of the last units to leave Richmond later wrote:

> The roaring and crackling of the burning houses, the trampling and snorting of our horses over the paved streets as we swept along, wild sounds of every description, while the rising sun came dimly through the cloud of smoke that hung like a pall around him, makes up a scene that beggars description, and which I hope never to see

The ruins of Richmond, Virginia, soon after its capture by Union troops. Robert E. Lee ordered military supplies and strategic materials, such as cotton, burned the night of April 2, 1865, to keep them from falling into Union hands. The fires got out of control and burned down much of the city.

again—the saddest of many of the sad sights of war—a city undergoing pillage at the hands of it own mob, while the standards of an empire were taken from its capitol, and the tramp of a victorious enemy at its gates.

A dramatic symbolic end to the siege of Richmond occurred on April 3. Richmond had a special visitor— Abraham Lincoln. Accompanied by his son Tad, Admiral David Porter, and about a dozen sailors, Lincoln had come to take a look at the city that had been the Confederate capital. Lincoln's group arrived before most of the Union troops who were on their way to occupy the city. Virtually all white residents of the city stayed inside. Masses of black people came out to see Lincoln, however. Lincoln's visit that day also included a trip to the Confederate White

House, where he sat at Jefferson Davis's desk.

Meanwhile, Grant was busy pursuing Lee. He had decided that the best move was not to chase Lee, but rather to try to get in front of the Confederates. Lee was traveling toward Amelia Court House, where he hoped to unite the five strands of his army and pick up supplies. A second store of rations was waiting at Danville, farther to the west. Lee and his men were in for an unpleasant shock on April 4, when they reached Amelia Court House. There were plenty of train cars, as promised, but the train cars were filled with artillery equipment and ammunition—not the food the army desperately needed. The nearby countryside was unable to help. It had been stripped of food the winter before. With the Union army closing in, Lee and the Confederate troops would have to leave quickly.

On April 6, the Union VI Corps and cavalry caught up to Confederate forces under Richard Ewell and Richard Anderson at Sayler's Creek. In a battle that started in the late afternoon, this section of Lee's army was nearly destroyed. Ewell himself, along with Lee's son General G.W.C. Lee, were among the Confederate prisoners. The next day, despite the disaster, Lee politely rejected a message from Grant asking the Confederate army to surrender.

On the morning of April 9, Union forces got ahead of Lee at a small hamlet called Appomattox Court House. At Lee's instructions, John Gordon's men staged one final attack. They brushed aside Union cavalry, and then saw what was behind the cavalry—three full-strength Union infantry corps, which outnumbered Lee's entire army. The rest of the Union army was closing in on Lee from the east. The way to the north was open, but the only option in that direction would be for the army to disperse and try to fight as partisans. Lee rejected this option, which promised more bloodshed.

It took nearly four years—April 12, 1861 to April 2, 1865—from the firing on Fort Sumter for Richmond and

Selected Civil War Casualties

BATTLE	UNION CASUALTIES				CONFEDERATE CASUALTIES[1]			
	KILLED	WOUNDED	MISSING[2]	TOTAL	KILLED	WOUNDED	MISSING	TOTAL
1st Bull Run July 21, 1861	491	1,011	1,216	2,708	387	1,582	12	1,981
Antietam September 17, 1861	2,108[3]	9,549	753	12,390	2,700	9,024	1,800	13,524
Fredericksburg December 13, 1862	1,284	9,600	1,769	12,653	595	4,061	653	5,309
Chancellorsville May 1–4, 1863	1,575	9,594	5,676	16,792	1,665	9,081	2,018	12,764
Gettysburg July 1–3, 1864	3,155	14,529	5,365	23,049	3,903	18,735	5,425	28,063
Wilderness May 5–7, 1864	2,246	12,137	3,383	17,666	1,123[4]			
Cold Harbor June 1–3, 1864				12,000[5]	Confederate figures not available.			
Petersburg initial assaults June 15–30, 1864	2,013	9,935	4,612	16,569	Estimated dead for Hill's corps and Field and Kershaw's divisions—2,970			
The Crater July 30, 1864	419	1,679	1,910	4,008				1,200
Cedar Creek October 19, 1864	644	3,430	1,591	5,665	320	1,540	1,050	2,910
Petersburg April 2, 1864	296	2,565	500	3,361	Estimated 3,000 prisoners. Figures for killed, wounded, and non-captured missing not available			
Appomattox campaign March 29–April 9, 1865	711	3,250	556	4,517	No breakdown of losses. Lee's technical casualty rate was 100 percent with the surrender of 27,800 men at Appomattox.			

[1] All Civil War casualties are estimates to some degree, because of faulty record-keeping. Few reports of Confederate casualties exist for the last year of the Civil War.

[2] Missing is a category that includes captured, not yet confirmed as killed, and not returned to unit.

[3] Some estimates put Antietam casualty figures, particular the dead, as much as 20% higher.

[4] Complete Confederate figures are not available. This is the writer's estimate. The figure is likely a bit low.

[5] Figures not complete. Estimates are that roughly 2,000 Union soldiers were killed in the main attack on June 2, 1864.

Note: General estimates of dead from the Civil War are 625,000 on both sides. This consists of roughly one-third killed in battle or dead of wounds. Two-thirds died of disease. World War I, 1914–1918, was the first war in which more soldiers died in action than of disease.

General Robert E. Lee is shown at his home in Richmond, a few days after he surrendered his army at Appomattox. To the left of the photo is Lee's oldest son, Major General Custis Lee; to the right is Lee's aide, Colonel Walter Taylor. Lee did not want to pose for this and several other photos, taken by Matthew Brady or one of his assistants, but was persuaded by his son and by Colonel Taylor.

Petersburg to fall to Union forces. One week later, at 3:00 P.M. on April 9, 1865, 75 miles (121 kilometers) to the west of Petersburg, at Appomattox Court House, Lee surrendered the Army of Northern Virginia to Ulysses S. Grant. The Civil War had finally come to an end.

1861

April 12–13	Firing on Fort Sumter; Fort Sumter evacuated April 15, 1861.
July 21	Battle of Bull Run, first major battle of Civil War.

1862

April 5–May 3	Union siege of Yorktown, Virginia.
April 6–7	Battle of Shiloh, Tennessee.
September 17	Battle of Antietam, Maryland.
December 13	Battle of Fredericksburg, Virginia.

1863

May 1–4	Battle of Chancellorsville, Virginia.

December 13, 1862
Battle of Fredericksburg, Virginia.

July 1–3, 1863
Battle of Gettysburg, Pennsylvania.

April 12–13, 1861
Firing on Fort Sumter; Fort Sumter evacuated April 15, 1861.

May 1–4, 1863
Battle of Chancellorsville, Virginia.

1861

1863

September 17, 1862
Battle of Antietam, Maryland.

May 18–July 4, 1863
Siege of Vicksburg, Mississippi.

Timeline

July 1–3	Battle of Gettysburg, Pennsylvania.
May 18–July 4	Siege of Vicksburg, Mississippi.
November 23–25	Battle of Chattanooga, Tennessee.

1864

May 5–6	Battle of the Wilderness, Virginia; Grant's 40 Days Campaign begins.
June 2	Battle of Cold Harbor.
June 15–19	Initial attacks at Petersburg, Virginia; siege of Petersburg begins.
June 20–30	Cavalry and infantry attacks on the Weldon Railroad.
July 12–13	Skirmishing at Fort Stevens, Washington, D.C.

July 12–13, 1864
Skirmishing at Fort Stevens, Washington, D.C.

April 2, 1865
Siege of Petersburg ends.

May 5–6, 1864
Battle of the Wilderness, Virginia; Grant's 40 Days Campaign begins.

July 30, 1864
Mine explosion and Battle of the Crater at Petersburg, Virginia.

April 9, 1865
Army of Northern Virginia surrenders at Appomattox Court House, Virginia.

1864   **1866**

June 15–19, 1864
Initial attacks at Petersburg, Virginia; siege of Petersburg begins.

April 1, 1865
Battle of Five Forks.

November 1864 – March 1865
Major actions slow down.

July 28–September 2	Siege of Atlanta, Georgia.
July 30	Mine explosion and Battle of the Crater at Petersburg, Virginia.
August 25	Attack on Ream's Station by Army of the Potomac.
November 1864–March 1865	Major actions slow down.

1865

March 25	Battle of Fort Stedman, Petersburg, Virginia.
March 31	Battles of Boydton Road, White Oak Road, and Dinwiddie Court House.
April 1	Battle of Five Forks.
April 2	Siege of Petersburg ends.
April 3	Union forces enter Richmond, Virginia.
April 9	Army of Northern Virginia surrenders at Appomattox Court House, Virginia.

TITLE PAGE: "Active and continuous . . ." July 22, 1865, Report of Lieut. Gen. Ulysses S. Grant, U.S. Army, Commanding Armies of the United States, including operations March 1864–May 1865, *Official Records of the War of the Rebellion* (OR), Washington, D.C.: Government Printing Office, 1880–1900, Series I, vol. XXXVI, Part I, p. 12.

CHAPTER 1, THE SIEGE OPENS

Page 7: "Never had the army . . ." Bruce Catton, *The Army of the Potomac: Volume III, A Stillness at Appomattox* (Garden City, NY: Doubleday and Company, 1951, 1962), p. 186.

Page 8: "The course Grant had determined . . ." Noah Andre Trudeau, *The Last Citadel* (Boston: Little, Brown and Company, 1991), p. 16.

Page 9: "Our forces will commence . . ." OR, Series I, vol. XL Part 1, p. 12.

Page 11: "Put us into it, Hancock . . ." Quoted in Bruce Catton, *The Army of the Potomac: Volume III, A Stillness at Appomattox* (Garden City, NY: Doubleday and Company, 1951, 1962), p. 191.

Pages 11: "The rage of the enlisted men . . ." Frank Wilkeson, *Recollections of a Private Soldier in the Army of the Potomac* (New York: G. P. Putnam's Sons, 1887), p. 162.

Page 11: "Petersburg at that hour . . ." G. T. Beauregard, "Four Days at Petersburg," *The Way to Appomattox: Battles and Leaders of the Civil War*, Robert Underwood Johnson and Clarence Clough Bell, eds., vol. IV (New York: Castle Books, 1956), p. 541.

Page 15: "Somewhere in the strained . . ." Trudeau, p. 53.

CHAPTER 2, GETTING TO PETERSBURG

Page 19: "It is impossible to conceive . . ." Theodore Irving, *More Than Conqueror: Memorials of J. Howard Kitching* (New York: Hurd and Houghton, 1873), p. 2.

Page 25: "not a striking man . . ." George Gordon Meade, ed., *Life and Letters of George Gordon Meade, Major General, United States Army* (New York: Charles Scribner's Sons, 1913), vol. II, p. 191.

Page 25: "A general who never got drunk . . ." Bruce Catton, *The Army of the Potomac: Volume III, A Stillness at Appomattox* (Garden City, NY: Doubleday and Company, Inc., 1953), p. 43.

Page 25: "That man [Grant] will fight us . . ." Horace Porter, *Campaigning with Grant* (New York: The Century Company, 1897), pp. 46–47.

Pages 26: " From an early period . . ." July 22, 1865, Report of Lieut. Gen. Ulysses S. Grant, U.S. Army, Commanding Armies of the United States, including operations March 1864–May 1865, *Official Records of the War of the Rebellion* (Washington, D.C.: Government Printing Office, 1880–1900), Series I, vol. XXXVI, Part I, p. 12.

Page 29: "With my staff and a small escort . . ." Ulysses S. Grant, *Personal Memoirs of U.S. Grant* (New York: Charles L. Webster & Company, 1886), vol. II, p. 210.

Page 29: "In the winter of 1863–1864 . . ." Noah Andre Trudeau, "The Walls of 1864," *With My Face to the Enemy: Perspectives on the Civil War*, ed. Robert Crowley (New York: G. P. Putnam's Sons, 2001), pp. 413–428.

Page 30: "We must destroy this army . . ." J. William Jones, *Life and Letters of Robert E. Lee, Soldier and Man* (Washington, D.C.: The Neale Publishing Company, 1906), p. 50.

CHAPTER 3, THE FIRST MONTH

Page 35: "I have just seen your dispatch . . ." Carl Van Doren, ed., *The Literary Works of Abraham Lincoln* (New York: The Heritage Press, 1942), p. 268.

Page 41:   "So unexpected was this attack . . ."
Noah Andre Trudeau, *The Last Citadel*
(Boston: Little, Brown and Company,
1991), p. 73.

Page 42:   "The affair was a stampede . . ."
Andrew A. Humphreys, *The Virginia
Campaign of '64 and '65* (New York:
Charles Scribner's Sons, 1908), p. 229.

Page 45:   "The damage to the enemy . . ."
July 22, 1865, Report of Lieut.
Gen. Ulysses S. Grant, U.S. Army,
Commanding Armies of the United
States, including operations March
1864–May 1865, *Official Records
of the War of the Rebellion* (Washing-
ton, D.C.: Government Printing
Office, 1880–1900), OR, Series I, Vol.
XXXVI, Part 1, p. 23.

CHAPTER 4, DIGGING A MINE

Page 47:   "We could blow that damned fort . . ."
Quoted in Bruce Catton, *The Army of
the Potomac: Volume III, A Stillness at
Appomattox* (Garden City, NY: Doubleday and Company, Inc., 1953), p. 220.

Page 48:   "Get down, you fool." Frank E. Vandiver,
Jubal's Raid (Westport, CT: Green-
wood Press, Publishers, 1960), p. 168.

Page 52:   "We could blow that damned fort . . ."
Quoted in Catton, p. 220.

Page 52:   "assented" Andrew A. Humphreys,
The Virginia Campaign of '64 and '65
(New York: Charles Scribner's Sons,
1908), p. 250.

Page 53:   "The ground on our side . . ." Ibid.

Page 53:   "The mine as a means . . ." *Official
Records of the War of the Rebellion*
(Washington, D.C.: Government
Printing Office, 1880–1900), Series I,
Vol. XL, Part 1, p. 76.

Page 55:   "It was noticed that . . ." Gary W.
Gallagher, ed., *Fighting for the
Confederacy: The Personal Recollections
of General Edward Porter Alexander*
(Chapel Hill and London: University
of North Carolina Press, 1989),
pp. 442–443.

Page 55:   "They were coming, but . . ." Ibid.,
p. 445.

Page 58:   "The Army of the Potomac was led . . ."
Catton, p. 238.

Pages 58–59:   "I understood that they . . ." *Official
Records*, Series I, Vol. XL, Part 1,
p. 47.

CHAPTER 5, THE BATTLE OF THE CRATER

Page 61:   "Such opportunity for carrying . . ."
Quoted in William S. McFeely,
Grant: A Biography (New York
and London: W. W. Norton &
Company, 1981), p. 179.

Page 62:   "This operation which . . ." *Official
Records of the War of the Rebellion*
(Washington, D.C.: Government
Printing Office, 1880–1900), Series I,
Vol. 40, Part 1, p. 47.

Page 63:   "It was a magnificent spectacle . . ."
Noah Andre Trudeau, *The Last
Citadel* (Boston: Little, Brown and
Company, 1991), p. 109.

Page 63:   "a monstrous tongue of flame . . ."
Major William H. Powell, "The
Battle of the Petersburg Crater,"
*The Way of Appomattox, Battles
and Leaders of the Civil War,
Volume IV*, Robert Underwood
Johnson and Clarence Clough
Buel, eds. (New York: Castle
Books, 1956), p. 551.

Pages 67:   "With the notable exception . . ."
Powell, p. 560.

Page 69:   "The loss in the disaster . . ."
Official Records, Series I, vol. 40,
part 1, p. 17.

**CHAPTER 6, ANOTHER LARGE EXPLOSION
AND SOME OFFENSIVE MOVES**

Page 73:   "Had our own troops behaved . . ."
Orlando B. Wilcox, Brevet Major-
General, U.S.A., "Actions on the
Weldon Railroad," *The Way of
Appomattox, Battles and Leaders of
the Civil War, Volume IV*, Robert
Underwood Johnson and Clarence
Clough Buel, eds. (New York:
Castle Books, 1956), p. 573.

Page 77:   "a staggering scene, a mass . . ."
             Noah Andre Trudeau, *The Last Citadel*
             (Boston: Little, Brown and Company,
             1991), p. 139.

Page 77:   "Which vividly recalled . . ." General
             Horace Porter, *Campaigning with
             Grant* (New York: The Centry
             Company, 1897), p. 273.

Page 79:   "I told him that . . ." Ibid., p. 275.

Page 80:   "On the 11th orders . . ." Henrietta
             Stratton Jacquette, ed., *South After
             Gettysburg: Letters of Cornelia Hancock,
             1863–1868* (New York: Thomas Y.
             Crowell Company, 1937 and 1956), p. 143.

Page 80:   "Suffocatingly hot to-night . . ."
             Trudeau, p. 147.

Page 86:   "With all our starvation . . ."; "I have
             since I . . ." Noah Andre Trudeau,
             The Last Citadel (Boston: Little,
             Brown and Company, 1991), p. 258.

Page 87:   "This morning, as for some days past . . ."
             Stephen B. Oates, *With Malice Toward
             None: The Life of Abraham Lincoln*
             (New York: A Mentor Book, 1977),
             p. 429.

CHAPTER 7, THE WINTER

Page 89:   "When I see and hear . . ." John Rozier,
             ed., *The Granite Farm Letters: The Civil
             War Correspondence of Edgeworth and
             Sallie Bird* (Athens, GA: 1988), p. 211.

Page 93:   "a young mother, beautiful . . ." Mary
             A. H. Gay, *Life in Dixie During the War*
             (Atlanta: DeKalb Historical Society,
             1979), pp. 208–209.

Page 93–94:   "To those who reflected . . ." Sallie
             Brock Putman, *Richmond During the
             War: Four Years of Personal Observation*
             (Lincoln and London: University of
             Nebraska Press, 1966), p. 351.

Page 94:   "Richmond was now . . ." Ibid., p. 352.

CHAPTER 8, END GAME

Page 99:   "Lieutenant-General Grant . . ."
             Carl Van Doren, ed., *The Literary
             Works of Abraham Lincoln* (New York:
             The Heritage Press, 1942), p. 276.

Page 101:   "This force is in more danger . . ."
             General Horace Porter, *Campaigning
             with Grant* (New York: Da Capo
             Press, 1988), p. 432.

Page 104:   "This was the first time . . ." Bruce
             Catton, *The Army of the Potomac:
             Volume III, A Stillness at Appomattox*
             (Garden City, NY: Doubleday and
             Company, Inc., 1953), p. 358.

Page 105:   "The roaring and crackling . . ."
             Edward M. Boykin, Lieutenant
             Colonel, 7th South Carolina Cavalry,
             The Falling Flag (New York:
             E. J. Hale and Son, Publishers, 1874), pp.
             12–13.

Andrews, Eliza Frances. *The Wartime Journal of a Georgia Girl*. New York: D. Appleton and Company, 1908.

Boykin, Edward. *The Falling Flag*. New York: E. J. Hale and Sons, Publishers, 1874.

Catton, Bruce. *The Army of the Potomac: Volume III, A Stillness at Appomattox*. Garden City, NY: Doubleday and Company, 1953.

Forsyth, Harry L. *Sixty Days*. Freeman, SD: Pine Hill Press, 1997.

Gallagher, Gary W., ed. *Fighting for the Confederacy: The Personal Recollections of General Edward Porter Alexander*. Chapel Hill and London: University of North Carolina Press, 1989.

Gay, Mary A. H. *Life in Dixie During the War*. Atlanta: DeKalb Historical Society, 1979.

Grant, Ulysses S. *Personal Memoirs of U.S. Grant*. New York: Charles L. Webster & Company, 1886.

Howe, Thomas J. *The Petersburg Campaign: Wasted Valor*. Lynchburg, VA: H. E. Howard, Inc., 1988.

Humphreys, Andrew A. *The Virginia Campaign of '64 and '65*. New York: Charles Scribner's Sons, 1908.

Irving, Theodore. *More than Conquerer: Memorials of J. Howard Kitching*. New York: Hurd and Houghton, 1873.

Jacquette, Henrietta Stratton, ed. *South after Gettysburg: Letters of Cornelia Hancock, 1863–1868*. New York: Thomas Y. Crowell Company, 1937, 1956.

Johnson, Robert Underwood, and Clarence Clough Bell, eds. *The Way to Appomattox: Battles and Leaders of the Civil War*, vol. IV. New York: Castle Books, 1956 reprint.

Lincoln, Abraham. *The Literary Works of Abraham Lincoln*. Selected, with an introduction, by Carl Van Doren, New York: The Heritage Press, 1942.

Livermore, Thomas L. *Numbers & Losses in the Civil War in America: 1861–1865*. Bloomington: Indiana University Press, 1957.

McFeely, William S. *Grant: A Biography*. New York and London: W. W. Norton & Company, 1981.

Meade, George Gordon, ed. *Life and Letters of George Gordon Meade, Major General, United States Army*. New York: Charles Scribner's Sons, 1913.

Oates, Stephen B. *With Malice Toward None: The Life of Abraham Lincoln*. New York: A Mentor Book, 1977.

Phisterer, Frederick. *Statistical Record of the Armies of the United States*. New York: Charles Scribner's Sons, 1907.

Porter, Horace. *Campaigning with Grant*. New York: The Century Company, 1897.

Putnam, Sallie Brock. *Richmond During the War: Four Years of Personal Observation*. Lincoln and London: University of Nebraska Press, 1966.

Sears, Stephen W. *To the Gates of Richmond: The Peninsula Campaign*. New York:

Ticknor & Fields, 1992.

Sword, Wiley. *Southern Invincibility: A History of the Confederate Heart*. New York: St. Martin's Press, 1999.

Trudeau, Noah Andre. "The Walls of 1864," in Robert Crowley, ed., *With My Face to the Enemy: Perspectives on the Civil War*. New York: G. P. Putnam's Sons, 2001.

————. *The Last Citadel*. Boston: Little, Brown and Company, 1991.

United States Government, War Department. *The War of the Rebellion: A Compilation of the Official Records of the Union and Confederate Armies*. Washington, D.C.: Government Printing Office, 1880–1900.

Vandiver, Frank E. *Jubal's Raid*. Westport, CT: Greenwood Press, Publishers, 1960.

Wilkeson, Frank. *Recollections of a Private Soldier in the Army of the Potomac*. New York: G. P. Putnam's Sons, 1887.

Winik, Jay. *April 1865*. New York: HarperCollins, Publishers, 2001.

Catton, Bruce. *The Army of the Potomac: Mr. Lincoln's Army*. Garden City, New York: Doubleday and Company, 1951, 1962.

————. *The Army of the Potomac: Glory Road*. Garden City, NY: Doubleday and Company, 1952.

Crowley, Robert, ed. *With My Face to the Enemy: Perspectives on the Civil War*. New York: G. P. Putnam's Sons, 2001.

Davis, William C. *An Honorable Defeat*. New York: Harcourt, Inc., 2001.

Keegan, John. *Fields of Battle: The Wars for North America*. New York: Vintage Books, 1997.

Latimer, Jon. *Deception in War*. New York: The Overlook Press, 2001.

McPherson, James M. *Battle Cry of Freedom: The Civil War Era*. New York and Oxford: Oxford University Press, 1988.

Weigley, Russell F. *A Great Civil War*. Bloomington and Indianapolis: Indiana University Press, 2000.

page:

6:   AP/Wide World
10: Hulton Archive
15: AP/Department of Defense
18: Hulton Archive
24: AP/Wide World
27: AP/Wide World
31: Hulton Archive
34: Hulton Archive
39: Medford Historical Society
     Collection/Corbis
43: AP/Wide World
46: AP/Wide World
54: Corbis
57: Reprint Battler and Leaders
     of the Civil War, 1958
60: Corbis

65: Medford Historical Society
     Collection/Corbis
69: Courtesy Eastern Publication
70: Corbis
72: Bettmann/Corbis
78: AP/Wide World
82: Medford Historical Society
     Collection/Corbis
85: Corbis
88: Courtesy Eastern Publication
93: Medford Historical Society
     Collection/Corbis
98: Hulton Archive
103: Hulton Archive
106: Courtesy Eastern Publication
109: Bettmann/Corbis

frontis: National Park Service

BRUCE L. BRAGER has worked for many years as a staff or freelance writer/editor, specializing in history, political science, foreign policy, energy, and defense/military topics. This is his third book, his second book for young adults. His previous book is The Texas 36th Division: A History, (published 2002), a study of a military unit from 2836 to the present. Brager has published over 50 articles for the general and specialized history markets, the bulk of them on the American Civil War. He was raised in the Washington, D.C. area and New York City. Brager graduated from the George Washington University, and currently lives in Arlington, Virgina.

TIM McNEESE is an Associate Professor of History at York College in Nebraska. He is the author of more than fifty books and educational materials on everything from Egyptian pyramids to American Indians. Professor McNeese graduated from York College with his Associate of Arts degree, as well as Harding University where he received his Bachelor of Arts degree in history and political science. He received his Master of Arts degree in history from Southwest Missouri State University. His audiences range from elementary students to adults. He is currently in his 27th year of teaching. Professor McNeese's writing career has earned him a citation in the "Something About the Author" reference work. He is married to Beverly McNeese who teaches English at York College.